Visible Signs

Also by Lawrence Raab

The Probable World

•

What We Don't Know About Each Other

•

Other Children

•

The Collector of Cold Weather

•

Mysteries of the Horizon

Visible Signs

NEW AND SELECTED POEMS

Lawrence Raab

PENGUIN POETS

PENGUIN BOOKS
Published by the Penguin Group
Penguin Putnam Inc., 375 Hudson Street, New York, New York 10014, U.S.A.
Penguin Books Ltd, 80 Strand, London WC2R 0RL, England
Penguin Books Australia Ltd, 250 Camberwell Road, Camberwell, Victoria 3124, Australia
Penguin Books Canada Ltd, 10 Alcorn Avenue, Toronto, Ontario, Canada M4V 3B2
Penguin Books India (P) Ltd, 11 Community Centre, Panchsheel Park, New Delhi - 110 017, India
Penguin Books (N.Z.) Ltd, Cnr Rosedale and Airborne Roads, Albany, Auckland, New Zealand
Penguin Books (South Africa) (Pty) Ltd, 24 Sturdee Avenue, Rosebank, Johannesburg 2196, South Africa

Penguin Books Ltd, Registered Offices:
Harmondsworth, Middlesex, England

First published in Penguin Books 2003

1 3 5 7 9 10 8 6 4 2

Mysteries of the Horizon (Doubleday). Copyright © Lawrence Raab, 1969, 1971, 1972
"Voices Answering Back: The Vampires" and "Magritte: The Song of the Glass Keys and the Cape of Storms" first appeared in *The American Scholar*; and "To Lorca" in *Shenandoah*. Excerpts from "Somnabule Ballad," translated by Stephen Spender and J. L. Gili from *The Selected Poems of Federico Garcia Lorca*, edited by Francisco Garcia Lorca and Donald M. Allen. Copyright 1955 by New Directions Publishing Corporation. Reprinted by permission of New Directions Publishing Corporation. Excerpt from "Seven Charms for a New Day" from *In the Trail of the Wind*, edited by John Bierhorst, Farrar, Straus & Giroux, Inc.

The Collector of Cold Weather (Ecco Press). Copyright © Lawrence Raab, 1973, 1974, 1975, 1976
"Visiting the Oracle" first appeared in *The New Yorker*; "Water" in *Shenandoah*; "The Assassin's Fatal Error" in *The American Scholar*; "Attack of the Crab Monsters" in *Berkshire Review*; "Doctor Watson's Final Case" in *Marilyn*; and "The Blue Histories of the Wind" in *Prairie Schooner*.

Other Children (Carnegie Mellon University Press, 1987)
All the selections from this volume are reprinted by permission of Carnegie Mellon University Press.

What We Don't Know About Each Other (Penguin Books). Copyright © Lawrence Raab, 1993
"A Crow," "What He Thought About the Party," "Stories in Which the Past Is Made," "At Evening," "Marriage," and "The Secret Life" first appeared in *Poetry*; "What We Don't Know About Each Other" and "What I Forgot to Mention" in *The New Yorker*; "Lies," "The Shakespeare Lesson" and "Happiness" in *The Kenyon Review*; "Learning How to Write" in *Salmagundi*; "The Bad Muse" in *The Journal*; "The Sudden Appearance of a Monster at a Window" in *The Denver Quarterly*; "The Uses of Nostalgia" and "Daily Life" in *Virginia Quarterly Review*; and "Magic Problems" in *Shenandoah*. Reprinted by permission of Penguin Books.

The Probable World (Penguin Books). Copyright © Lawrence Raab, 2000
"Why the Truth Is Hidden" first appeared in *The Journal*; "Love," "Hunters," "False Nocturne," and "My Spiritual Life" in *The Gettysburg Review*; "Respect" and "My Life at the Movies" in *The New Republic*; "A Small Lie" in *The Kenyon Review*; "All Day" in *Antaeus*; "The Lost Things" in *Poetry*; "Why Tragedy Is the Wrong Word" in *Prairie Schooner*; "Years Later" and "The Best Days" in *The New England Review*; "My Soul Is a Light Housekeeper" in *The New Yorker*; "Another Argument About the Impossible" in *River Styx*; "Permanence" and "The Questions Poems Ask" in *Virginia Quarterly Review*; "My Life Before I Knew It" in *Salmagundi*; and "The Invisible" and "Fragile" in *Crab Orchard Review*. Reprinted by permission of Penguin Books.

Acknowledgments continue on p. ix.

LIBRARY OF CONGRESS CATALOGING IN PUBLICATION DATA
Raab, Lawrence, 1946–
Visible signs : new and selected poems / Lawrence Raab.
p. cm.
ISBN 0 14 20.0269 0
I. Title.
PS3568 A2 V57 2003
811'.54—dc21   2002035481

PRINTED IN THE UNITED STATES OF AMERICA
Set in Adobe Caslon with Jante Antiqua Demi and AGWile Roman Black
Designed by Sabrina Bowers

For Judy and Jenny
and for Jonathan Aaron

Grateful acknowledgent is made to the following magazines in which some of the new poems first appeared: *The Georgia Review*, "Damage"; *The Gettysburg Review*, "Miles Davis on Art" and "The End of the World"; *New England Review*, "Vanishing Point"; *The New Republic*, "Saint Augustine's Dog"; *The New Yorker*, "In Dreams"; *Organica*, "Dark Matter" and "Request"; *The Paris Review*, "Why It Often Rains in the Movies"; *Quarterly West*, "Some of the Things My Mother Said"; *River Styx,* "Small Ghost Poem"; *Virginia Quarterly Review*, "Camouflage," "Saint George's Dragon," and "The Invisible Hand"; *Witness*, "Talking to the Dog." "Rube Goldberg's Flower" was written for the catalogue of the exhibition, "Chain Reaction: Rube Goldberg and Contemporary Art."

Only minor changes have been made in a few of the selected poems, with the exception of "The Blue Histories of the Wind," which is printed here in a version substantially different from the one published in *The Collector of Cold Weather.*

I would like to thank Yaddo, The MacDowell Colony, The Peter S. Reid Foundation, and Williams College for their generous support.

Music, states of happiness, mythology, faces scored by time, certain twilights, certain places, all want to tell us something, or told us something we should not have missed, or are about to tell us something. —JORGE LUIS BORGES

Things don't change, but by and by our wishes change.
—MARCEL PROUST

Contents

From *What We Don't Know About Each Other*

From *The Probable World*

New Poems

Why It Often Rains in the Movies

Because so much consequential thinking
happens in the rain. A steady mist
to recall departures, a bitter downpour
for betrayal. As if the first thing
a man wants to do when he learns his wife
is sleeping with his best friend, and has been
for years, the very first thing
is *not* to make a drink, and drink it,
and make another, but to walk outside
into bad weather. It's true
that the way we look doesn't always
reveal our feelings. Which is a problem
for the movies. And why somebody has to smash
a mirror, for example, to show he's angry
and full of self-hate, whereas actual people
rarely do this. And rarely sit on benches
in the pouring rain to weep. Is he wondering
why he didn't see it long ago? Is he wondering
if in fact he did, and lied to himself?
And perhaps she also saw the many ways
he'd allowed himself to be deceived. In this city
it will rain all night. So the three of them
return to their houses, and the wife
and her lover go upstairs to bed
while the husband takes a small black pistol
from a drawer, turns it over in his hands,
then puts it back. Thus demonstrating
his inability to respond to passion
with passion. But we don't want him
to shoot his wife, or his friend, or himself.
And we've begun to suspect

that none of this is going to work out,
that we'll leave the theater feeling
vaguely cheated, just as the movie,
turning away from the husband's sorrow,
leaves him to be a man who must continue,
day after day, to walk outside into the rain,
outside and back again, since now there can be
nowhere in this world for him to rest.

In Dreams

Sometimes, in a dream, I'll find myself
avoiding the reckless choices I would
in life also turn away from. And I'll think:
But this is a dream, you can do what you want.

But I can't, and even trying
to manage whatever loopy story
is tonight's production means I'm just
that much closer to waking up. Thus thought

is shown to be the enemy of action.
Which we knew already. I turn a corner,
certain I'm being followed. Pursued.
Chased by a vampire. Who keeps gaining on me

until I see these huge doors swinging open.
A concert's about to begin. I sit down
next to a beautiful woman. She turns to me
and smiles, and touches my arm. Then

I'm somewhere else, maybe it's her place.
She's unbuttoning her blouse, I'm telling her
I'm married, and my waking self is crying out—
No, no, don't do that! But it's too late,

she's gone. Do I feel virtuous?
Not even a little. What did she look like?
I don't remember. Like no one. But for a moment
I can feel the place where she touched me,

on my wrist, near the vein. In this way
the past returns, dressed up
as a ragged troupe of actors trapped
in their most famous roles. The callow youth.

The worried, untested knight.
The terrible monster. The beautiful woman
without mercy. Poor ghosts,
whose deepest wishes must be sleep.

Inside the Chateau:
A Pornographic Story

AFTER GEORGES BATAILLE

She had gone to search for me
inside the chateau, but first
she took off her clothes—to "feel more free,"
she told me when she found me, although
she didn't ask why I was also naked,
or why my hands were covered with blood.
When we looked for her dress she said
the wind must have carried it away.

This is what we knew: Everything we saw
aroused us. An empty room, a bowl
of milk, the moon like a blind eye,
the calling of the night birds.
The world kept urging us upon each other,
and we could no more resist than we could
will ourselves not to breathe. Did we ever
wish for that? We never said it.

Our lives were overwhelming. But not
in the way, reader, yours might be.
Money, for example, didn't concern us.
The German Count, the American millionaire—
they'd arrive when required, provide the car,
the boat, the next chateau. We took it all
for granted. I never wondered
why the past meant nothing to me.

I never felt inclined to read a book
when I could throw myself yet again
upon Simone or Marcelle. That was what
they needed me to do, what our author needed.
Thus the sight of eggs aroused Simone, the sight
of blood aroused us both, and the sign
of the cross drove us to destroy a priest,
until there was no question we were lost.

So lost we were free? I didn't think
about it. We were insatiable. We knew
the only exhaustion permitted us was death.
But the thought of death aroused us,
and we would rip off our clothes
if we were wearing any, fall into each other
on the wet grass outside the chateau
where, Simone, that night your dress was caught

in the upper branches of a tree.
It fluttered like a spirit, whether angry
or disappointed I couldn't tell,
since what I remember now I'm sure
I didn't notice at the time.
No doubt the wind took it away, hid it
deep in the forest, ashamed for us,
who were not allowed to feel regret.

The Invisible Hand

No, I just can't write today, I said
to myself, sprawling on the couch, my mind
an open invitation to sleep, when there it was:
The Invisible Hand. A title. Having arrived
unbidden, it felt like inspiration,

but like a movie as well, which troubled me.
Hadn't I written that poem already? I recognized
the brilliant scientist, whose inattention
to the world causes the accident that kills
his pretty fiancée, pushing him over the edge

and fixing all his genius on a single idea—
the reanimation of matter—until finally
she is yanked out of the dark nether-regions
where the dead live. And from which, he discovers,
they have no desire to return. Yes,

but how does the invisible hand come in?
It had to be literal. No hand of fate,
no impalpable guiding force, but actual flesh,
chopped off, then bandaged, and sometimes
(but not always) transparent. Once it might

have been attached to a famous musician,
so this hand knew beauty, but had learned
how to kill, and thus was torn
between those great forces that make war
in a man's soul. This wasn't a poem I had written,

but could a murderous, disembodied hand
really be the best approach? Then I was struck.
Had it been The Invisible *Man*? It was time
for lunch, and as I ate I thought. Soon
I'd take my dog, Molly, for a walk,

after which we'd drive to the Stop & Shop,
and so on through the rest of the afternoon
until the whole idea of an invisible hand
might begin to seem—as in fact
it already had—just a little silly.

And walking outside with Molly, the fields
around us lavishly green, the lilacs almost
unbearably rich, puffy white clouds
scooting through the sky, even the idea
of writing a poem felt like a project

better left to another day, a morning
with fewer distractions, quieter, when the wind
would not be bending the small trees so fiercely,
making them creak and shudder, as if touched,
and touched again, by everything I could not see.

Some of the Things My Mother Said

It'll never be noticed from a trotting horse,
my mother used to say. Which meant:
Forget about it, nobody's going to look
that close. Or else: We're late,
you don't have time to change your shirt.
And even: Try not to worry so much
about everything. But I did,
brooding and slouching around the house,
determined to resist any kind of advice.
Like being a little nicer to people,
my mother would suggest,
since then they'd be nicer to me.
Who could have used another friend or two.
Who needed to get out more, toss a ball around,
spend less time alone. Of course
I didn't listen. And now
I'm thinking of the life I'd have
if I could do it over: the wild cheers
of my friends when I'd make the catch
that wins the game, the way the girls
would smile at me and blush. And then
I'm sitting in my living room,
trophies on the mantle, the wife out shopping,
all the kids gone, remembering that game,
and other games, which look small
and far away, which don't feel
as important as they should. Sometimes
my mother would laugh and say,
You don't have the sense to come in
out of the rain. Which could have meant
exactly that: a friend and I were out there

in the backyard in the rain, just happy
to be tossing a ball around.
But she probably meant: You need to think
more carefully about what you're doing.
God in heaven, I can hear her saying.
Forget about it. Let it go.

Miles Davis on Art

"The only way to make art," Miles Davis
said, "is to forget what is unimportant."
That sounds right, although the opposite
also feels like the truth. Forget
what looks important, hope it shows up

later to surprise you. I understand
he meant you've got to clear
your mind, get rid of everything
that doesn't matter. But how can you tell?
Maybe the barking of a dog at night

is exactly what you need
to think about. "Just play within
the range of the idea,"
Charlie Parker said. The poem
that knows too quickly what's important

will disappoint us. And sometimes
when you talk about art
you mean it, sometimes you're just
fooling around. But once he had the melody
in place, he could leave it behind

and go where he wanted, trusting
the beautiful would come to him, as it may
to a man who's worked hard enough
to be ready for it. And he was,
more often than not. That was what he knew.

My Father Drives Away

My father was missing.
Had he been kidnapped?
Unlikely, the detective explained,
since no one had called
to demand a ransom.

Then he'd chosen to vanish?
Taken the convertible and gone off?
The detective said he was sorry,
but such things happened
more frequently than we would think.

And rarely did anyone
discover the reason,
or where the father ended up,
whether he was happy or ashamed,
or both. And that was it—

a small dream in which I knew
missing meant dead. And woke
before I could picture him in the car
with the top down and the radio on,
headed west, or south, wherever
I might have wanted him to be.

Letter

Today I did almost nothing.
Read a little, tried to write a sentence
to make another seem necessary.

I wasn't unhappy. Everything
I could will myself to do I'd done,
so I said I'd done enough.

Now I'm looking out my window:
white pine, ash, a single birch,
the leanings and crossings

of branches. And then the sky:
pale, undecided. Years ago
you wrote to me about a matter

that worried you, and you said
at the end, "That's probably the best,
and most true, way to think about it."

I kept your sentence in my notebook.
I liked its shape. I admired the way,
young as you were, you could feel

one kind of thinking
adjusting into another, one truth
becoming a better truth.

Now you're far off, and alone, and I
have no advice you haven't already
given yourself. What can I tell you?

That I'm here? That today, when I saw
how tenderly the light was moving
among those trees, I thought of you?

Tarantula

After the death of the sparrow
Fabre felt *a certain coolness*
at the evening meal. He could read
mute reproaches in the eyes of his family.

Jean-Henri Fabre (1823–1915):
celebrated French entomologist and author
of the ten-volume *Souvenirs Entomologiques.*
And the experiment—a tarantula
is made to bite the leg of a sparrow.

Almost immediately, Fabre notes,
the bird loses the use of that leg,
which drags, toes doubled in. Nevertheless,
he hops about on the other, seems well,
untroubled, hungry. Fabre's daughters
feed the sparrow flies, bread-crumbs,
apricot pulp. He eats, he clamors for food.

Yet the leg still drags. Temporary
paralysis, Fabre thinks, sure to disappear.
After two days the bird refuses to eat.
Wrapping himself in his stoicism
and his rumpled feathers, the Sparrow
hunches into a ball, now motionless,
now twitching. His daughters
cradle him in the hollows of their hands,
try to warm him with their breath.
The spasms become more frequent.

Thus that coolness at dinner,
which Fabre accepts. The experiment
causes pain, *the unspoken accusation
of cruelty.* He let them
take the bird in their hands.

How long will his daughters
hold this against him?
How long will they remember that sparrow,
poor victim of the curiosity of science?
The result in this case, he wrote,
seemed to me too dearly bought.

They forgave him, of course, and did not forget.

Vanishing Point

You're walking down a road
which someone has drawn to illustrate
the idea of perspective, and you are there
to provide a sense of scale.
See how the road narrows in the distance,
becoming a point at which
everything connects, or flies apart.
That's where you're headed.
The rest of the world is a blank page
of open space. Did you really think
you were just out for an aimless stroll?
And those mountains on the horizon:
the longer you look, the more forbidding
they become, bleak and self-important,
like symbols. But of what?
The future, perhaps. Destiny. Or the opposite.
The perpetual present, the foolishness of purpose.
At evening they recede into the sky
as if they had always been the sky.
Is it a relief to know you'll never reach them?
Is there any comfort in believing
you're needed where you are?

Winterset

The movie my mother and I had stayed up
late to watch ended with the young lovers
turning their backs on everything—
the lives their families expected them to choose,
all the certainties they could have planned on.

And the music told us this was right
because they had each other. I was twelve
or thirteen, had only dreamt
of such defiance, and so was hurt

when my mother said: Well, they'll find out
soon enough. I remember
the chairs we sat in, my surprise
at her dismissal of the moment.
Was she thinking of herself?

I couldn't have imagined it then.
I'd been moved by the light on their faces,
the music rising to enclose them,
all that false poetry. Perhaps

I've remembered it wrong.
Winterset. Was that the title?
She must have meant the world
was going to be hard on them, those kids,

since most of what they'd want
they couldn't have. And in time
love would begin to look like something else,
something bitter and irrevocable.
Or something ordinary

which they would learn to manage—
the kind of life
(she might have thought) you don't see
in the movies. Or think about
until it's yours.

Small Ghost Poem

Say it's the leaves, the way they rustle.
Say it's a shadow, the scraping of a stick.
Childhood friends, dead and buried—

they're out there now, small ghosts
who never knew when enough was enough.
One who ran into a car, one who tripped

on a stone and fell on a stick that poked
through his heart. Lost and forgotten,
they've gone into the world to become

the snap of a branch, the skittering
of leaves. What are they whispering?
It's late and it's cold. They want to come in.

Talking to the Dog

You can't say, I'm going away for a while
but I'll be back. When you say it
your wife calls from the next room,
"She's a dog—she doesn't understand."
Something's wrong is what she knows.
She wants to get in the car,
wants not to be left. Instead,
she refuses to look at you.
Is this sadness? Displeasure now,
sadness later? Or later only a room
with nobody in it, an odor, a noise,
the suspension of sleep.
She isn't thinking: Why has he left?
Was it my fault? She isn't a person.
She doesn't want to make you feel bad.

The End of the World

Just now, for no reason, I remembered
The Busy Bee, that restaurant we went to
sometimes on Fridays. Spaghetti and meatballs.
And my father would say, "So what do you think?
Can you eat all of that?" Back in my room

I'd stay up an extra hour, reading.
I loved the idea of traveling through time,
all the intricate tricks
of getting around another century
without leaving a trace—not even swatting

a fly, not even picking a flower,
or else the present isn't there
when you're ready to return.
I don't remember how I felt
about the end of the world, if I ever

thought of it actually happening:
all the missiles rising from their silos
and lunging off together,
some in our direction, a lot more
in theirs, hundreds of arcs

on the big maps the generals were watching.
Nothing could stop them. At school
we practiced hiding under our desks.
We were told not to look
into the light of the explosions.

When my parents decided
they wouldn't build a fallout shelter
I was upset, having pictured
a room for myself. Weren't they concerned?
But no one on our street had one.

Finally, my mother stacked a dozen jars
of fruit in the basement, announcing
that if it happened she wouldn't
be caught dead down there.
Was some madman yearning to press the button?

Did he have a plan? Anything
was possible, if you wanted
to worry about it. So the future unfolded,
and those jars of peaches and plums
remained on their shelves

long after my mother died—
emblems, furred with mold
and encased in dust. Like everything
that could have been different.
How easily we can make ourselves sad

just thinking. How little
that buys us. A night out, maybe.
A plate of spaghetti, too big to finish.

Dark Matter

Scientists at the University of Rome, according to The New York Times, *may have finally detected dark matter, the stuff that roughly eighty percent of the universe may be made of.*

Like certain superheroes, particles
of dark matter pass through other matter
unimpeded. But anti-gravity, scientists
explain, "still cannot be expected

to reverse the course of a falling apple,
or drive an inflating wedge of nothingness
between lovers." Which may be why
the hero works best alone.

Pals and sidekicks can be helpful,
but women are too curious, too quick
to believe the men they're with
must be, at heart, different men.

Of course they're right. And the hero
is in trouble if he doesn't
keep his other self a secret.
He wants to be in love, to offer

all the confidences a lover should.
But he has to save the world,
again and again. Thus it seems true
that a wedge of nothingness

divides the man and the woman,
but also that the falling of an apple
is irreversible.
The hero must expect evil

to continue. He cannot afford
to be surprised by strangeness.
Or ever expect a life in which
he could only be himself.

Camouflage

The poem that argues successfully against death
finds its place in the book you can buy
in stores that do not sell poetry.
If it's a bad poem, and it is,
does that really matter? Sorrow
doesn't want the truth, doesn't need
to think. *I know what you're feeling,*
the poem confides, whispering it
like a friend. Promises were made,
then broken. Exactly how did we expect
the world to work? Reality, Walker Evans said,
is not totally real. When I call
the Automated Flight Information System
I'm told: "It's okay to say 'I don't know.'"
But I don't. There are other ways
to check on a plane. A chickadee, trapped
beneath the plastic netting that keeps
the deer from eating our bushes, flutters
and thrashes. All she has to do
is let herself fall, then walk away.
If she were a person, and the net
a metaphor for other entanglements,
odds are she'd still be struggling.
At lunch my friend tells me he's spent
most of the morning looking for another word
for "camouflage." Disguise, cloak, mask.
He's tried them. Curtain, mantle, shade.
It's not the meaning. It's the context.
Maybe just the sound. If reality
isn't totally real, how real is it?
In an old anthology of poems, beside a line

about the wind rising over water and the dark
engulfing the trees, somebody's written:
Ah, too true! A sigh: truer than merely true.
Sadder than a fact. And this person
needed to write it down in the margin,
as if to tell me, leafing through
that book as a boy, what I didn't know.
Wind breaks the water's surface.
Evening falls. Nothing is only itself.

Damage

A woman tries to saw her leg off.
Before she can finish, she passes out.
She wakes up in the hospital, discovers
the leg's still there, makes
her next plan: railroad tracks, a train.

She doesn't want to die,
she wants to get rid of the leg,
which she hates. Nothing's wrong with it,
but when she looks in a mirror
the woman she sees has only one leg.

Nobody's shocked anymore to hear
about men who believe they're women,
women who need to be men.
Some people dream of themselves
without legs or arms. Some dream
of making love to those without legs
or arms. Some dream of watching.

Are these arguments against
the existence of God? Not if this
is what God likes to do—experiment
with the endless ways desire
can make us crazy. How easy it must be
to do that to people. Is there anything
someone hasn't wanted? So the woman

is happy to lie down in the dark
on the cold tracks, the train
blindly approaching—
and then the thought that really
this isn't going to work. And then

the voice she's heard once or twice before
tells her to be still, tells her
not to be afraid,
tells her she can hardly imagine
how beautiful she will be.

Saint George's Dragon

As such things go, my reign of terror
felt impressive.
I ate a lot of the town, was widely feared.
A few bloody rampages
taught them to bring my victims to me—
one a day, picked by chance. In exchange
I left their streets and shops alone,
found a cave out by the lake, settled in.
This princess George has rescued
meant nothing to me. Nobody did.
I understand
I have to be dragged around for a while now,
made to look dangerous, then dispatched.
George is brandishing his weapon,
showing off. And why not?
It's his moment. But what do you want
back there in the crowd?
You've known more than a couple
of the men I've eaten. You've been afraid
you might be next. Leashed and cowering,
do I remind you of an old dog
you used to kick around? Don't try
to feel sorry for me.
I'm getting what I deserve, and you're eager
to see it all and tell
the story: A single savage blow, green blood
leaping out. That sort of thing.
Good versus evil. After which
George goes off to become a saint, meaning
he gets to be dragged around and slaughtered
while the happy crowd congratulates itself.

And you are there.
Just let your tender feelings go
and be yourself. I'm the one
to whom you can do anything
and feel good about it afterwards. Let me be
the first of many.

Rube Goldberg's Flower

On a certain day you find yourself
walking down a street in a neighborhood
where every kind of misfortune is possible:
gaping manholes, grand pianos
tumbling from high buildings, gangsters

blasting away at each other.
But you're oblivious, a man
who's been struck by an idea—
the way the world might work
if it were given the chance

to take its time. The beauty
of a single task! How gracefully
it all unfolds above your head.
An immense apparatus
of accident and order.

Enthralled, you step across
the perilous hole, amble into a doorway
just as the bullets begin to fly,
then pause to consider
a small breeze, and so escape

the piano's conclusive descent.
How long, you wonder, should it take
to accomplish anything? How much
can be included in the process?
A pinwheel and a cord.

A trigger and an arrow. Flame.
Ice. A basin of water and a derby hat.
And a seal, a baby seal.
People will laugh, of course, blind
to such elegance, indifferent

to how well this system keeps the carnation
in your button-hole refreshed. Thus:
the breeze (A) touches the pinwheel (B),
winding the cord that pulls the trigger
that shoots the arrow (F), and so on through

(N) and (O) until the seal dives
into its basin and the water spills
onto the flower above your heart.
And if there is no breeze?
If there is no breeze

to start the pinwheel,
sneak up behind a bride and steal
a fresh flower. In her happiness
she will not begrudge you
a single blossom. And perhaps

she will even smile,
as if she hadn't noticed your thick glasses
or your impossible coat, or any of that
crazy contraption balanced
so precariously on your shoulders.

Saint Augustine's Dog

The story goes that Augustine was writing a letter
to ask Jerome about the state of the blessed
when a sudden light surprised him.
In the painting by Carpaccio you can see his pen
stuck in the air above the page, his head
tilted to the window, as he listens
to the voice of Jerome describing
his death and ascent to Christ. How rarely
are questions answered with such certainty.
Yet even a saint might feel bereft
for a while, unless for him
absence doesn't mean what it means
to most of us. So Augustine gazes out of his window
with an unreadable expression. And the painter
carefully keeps the miraculous from us—
no billowy figure floating through the sky, no sign
of an angel, only the light that could be
the light of any day. A cloud passes
from the face of the sun, and a man
working in his study might look up, arrested
by the unexpected and the ordinary,
while on the floor beside him his dog
is sitting, head tilted toward the vision,
or toward the man who might now be ready
to go outside for a walk. No reason,
the dog is thinking, to bark
or make a ruckus. Whatever
happens next will happen soon enough.

Request

For a long time I was sure
it should be "Jumping Jack Flash," then
the adagio from Schubert's C major Quintet,
but right now I want Oscar Peterson's

"You Look Good to Me." That's my request.
Play it at the end of the service,
after my friends have spoken.
I don't believe I'll be listening in,

but sitting here I'm imagining
you could be feeling what I'd like to feel—
defiance from the Stones, grief
and resignation with Schubert, but now

Peterson and Ray Brown are making
the moment sound like some kind
of release. Sad enough
at first, but doesn't it slide into

tapping your feet, then clapping
your hands, maybe standing up
in that shadowy hall in Paris
in the late sixties when this was recorded,

getting up and dancing
as I would not have done,
and being dead, cannot, but might
wish for you, who would then

understand what a poem—or perhaps only
the making of a poem, just that moment
when it starts, when so much
is still possible—

has allowed me to feel.
Happy to be there. Carried away.

from

Mysteries of the Horizon
(1972)

The Rules, The Story,
and the Way Out

The forests are crowded with deceptions,
perfect fruit glazed with a subtle poison.
Beware also of mirrors and masks.
But if the shoe fits, wear it.

If the sorcerer invites you to his
cottage in the country, remember
revelations are dangerous to ignore.
But if the coach comes apart, hang on.

You will discover the princess
by her good looks, and the prince likewise.
But if love cannot quicken their dreams,
you know where to turn.

You know, by now, the staleness of salt,
and the old tune of your heart enough to know
that it has not broken because
this story failed to include you.

Voices Answering Back:
The Vampires

Rising in lamplight dying at dawn
grim burials in sheds and cellars
the rats scuttling through holes
and the days following in their tracks
exiled here we named the hours
since you first forgot to be afraid
once departed we became
only ourselves
with the salt on our tongues
and the cold for company
so deft in escape so practiced in dying
you might have learned from us
but each time the easiest trick worked
the brandished cross the empty mirror
you could not see us our steps upon the stairs
and while you stumbled after bats in the garden
we climbed quietly
from the upstairs window down the drainpipe
and through all the parties
you never heard what we were saying
it was something about desire
what we had in common even then
in your silence you feared us
always winning at the end but do you think
nothing lingered past dawn
shadowed among the gathered elms
do not be mistaken
we heard you walking through our dreams
we felt death moving between your hands

now we are waking early
practicing with sunlight
now we pass unharmed beneath your terrible star
eyes covered hands in our pockets
for the rules have always said
if you stop believing in us
we inherit everything

Magritte: The Song of the Glass Keys and the Cape of Storms

There is no country
where you could not paint a street
and walk down it
or a door in a wall or a window
inside a window
to look out on the green horizon

The secrets of these places
are not concealed or explained

though single words have been inscribed
upon the surface of things
souvenirs of the hunters who turned
their faces into their hands
remembered by a stranger leaning over a stone bridge
beside a lion

Thus the covering of dreams unfolds
to show the lining and these keys—

a clock which is the wind
a valise which is a valise

No object is so fond of its name
that another cannot be found to live with it

The lives of saints and sleep
melt into each other

while the tuba is consumed with the Lord's fire

while solutions return to their questions without asking
and you arrange the relics of evening
on the table of this strict light

Through the door in the wall
through the window inside the window
through the silence

you carry the fact of the shoes
the fact of the wind and of the woman
the fact of the rain

Great clouds creep across the earth
and the storm falls into them like a song

To Lorca

Green, how much I want you green.
Green wind. Green branches.
The ship upon the sea
and the horse in the mountain.

Now the graves run all the way to the sea.
At this time of the year's turning even flowers
break. All the dying broods out of the land,
sits on top of boxes, forgets things,
and does not dream. Thirty times back
round your green sun, it was July that day
they came knocking. I do not know
the hour, but they left the grave unmarked.
Do you see the wound I have
from my breast to my throat? I see your face.
It is not easy to forget that face. All over a year
snow is descending, east and west hurrying down
like a storm of silence. I do not know
your season, yet that room you keep now
must be cold, with no quiet fire, and no book,
with all those priests gliding over you
and not knowing. No one,
not even you, could hear them moving.
But I am no more I, nor is my house
now my house. At the land's end cold water
climbs up the shore, and wants a bed,
and slips back. *Green, how much I want you green.*
Lorca, did they know it was you they shot?
The wind tears its eyes, and the snow
dries down into occupied ground. *Friend,*

I come bleeding. Your words
are the seeds we need still, though I imagine
your face tells us something
we must forget to live.

Seven Charms for a New Day

It was the wind that gave them life. It is the wind that comes out of our mouths now that gives us life. When this ceases to blow we die. In the skin at the tips of our fingers we see the trail of the wind; it shows us where the wind blew when our ancestors were created.

—NAVAJO POEM

1
Everywhere I discover the signs of ancestors

footprints lightly
lightly bending
this way
in new grass

2
Blue air opens around me
wind brushes my eyes   and wind again
enters the circles of my fingers

3
Inside the seed of the wind
children are born

Such a small place
but a heart can be lost in it

4
A tree rises from a familiar path
a white tree blossoming in a thorny road

What was lost has been here

and remains
kept close
in the rising of the light
in this sudden light rising
from the belly of a long and difficult night

5
Sleeping water stirs in the hollow of a rock
My face enters it my hands
tremble in it

Everything hides within itself
water inside water
flower inside flower

the bright seed inside the seed

6
I invent new signs in the fresh earth

The voices of birds will comfort me
The roots of unnamed plants will cure me
An amulet of stone will protect me
if I believe in it

7
And if I find you
at the end of the long falling of the wind

I will bend down
to touch your face

I will add my breath
like this
to yours

from

The Collector of Cold Weather
(1976)

Visiting the Oracle

It's dark on purpose
so just listen.

Maybe I inhabit a jar, maybe a pot,
maybe nothing. Only this
loose end of a voice
rising to meet you.
It sounds like water.
Don't think about that.

Let your servants climb back down the mountain
by themselves. I'll listen.
I'll tell you everything
I discover, but I can't
say what it means.

Someone will always
assure you of the best of fortunes,
but you know better.

And keep this in mind: The answer
reveals itself in time
like the clue that fits
perfectly and explains everything
after the crime has been solved.

Then you will say: *I should have known.*
It was there all along
and never even concealed,
like the story of the letter
overlooked by the thief because
it had not been hidden.
That's the trick, of course.

You don't need me.

Water

1

Whichever way water
turns it touches
itself turning in another direction

Invisible now
now reflecting whoever
finds himself looking
beneath the line of the wind

You remember the rules

Water seeks the level that pleases it
making a place for itself
wherever it chooses

calling everything
it touches its own
and falling back
in its own good time

2

Hundreds of feet beneath you
it creeps along a fault
drop by drop widening the rock
softening an edge
breaking off a splinter

So a cave blossoms

Water counts the time but does not care
You could learn from it
Speak to it of your troubles
Ask about your wound why it
refuses to heal

Ask about absence

Water has spent a long time learning
how to fill with itself
the space of a missing thing

3

Wherever it can go water goes

On your window
the early frost has drawn a map
and the small cloud of your breath
fades from the blade of the knife

The shape of someone like yourself
drifts in the shelter of still water
You reach down

A maze of circles meets your hand

The Assassin's Fatal Error

When in doubt have a man come through a door with a gun in his hand.
                              —RAYMOND CHANDLER

He comes through the door,
the big gun in his fist. He says
"Nobody's going anywhere."
Nobody was, nobody's
even here, except
me and this bottle of scotch,
and I'm used to waiting.

He tells me to explain
about the pearls, because he knows
ways to make me tell. However,
I know nothing about them,
nothing about Mr. R. or The Big Man,
and nothing about Oregon where I
have never lived at any time in my life.

Perhaps I'm lying, but he's convinced,
although he will shoot me anyway,
which I understand.

Perhaps I say, "What kept you?"
Probably I just finish the scotch,
which is third-rate but effective.

Mine, you understand, has been
a temporary disguise, which may or may not
be explained at a later time.

Its importance to the story
lies in the discovery of the body
by the detective, tomorrow.

I also turn up three chapters from the end
as a Doctor, where I can be trusted
even less than now, when I still have
this death to get through.

"There must be connections,"
I tell him. "There always are.
And it's smart to leave
the witness silent, get the job over,
and get out of town."

The gun wanders around the room.
"Listen," I tell him. "Anything
can happen. But this could be
the fatal error. You don't know
any more than I do."

The long tube of the silencer turns toward me.
I consider the finger on the trigger,
the sound like somebody coughing
upstairs in an old building,
and now the single bullet
suspended in the air between us.

You could ask: But what did I expect?
And I would have to say: Only this.
Nothing but this.

Attack of the Crab Monsters

Even from the beach I could sense it—
lack of welcome, lack of abiding life,
like something in the air, a certain
lack of sound. Yesterday
there was a mountain out there.
Now it's gone. And look

at this radio, each tube neatly
sliced in half. Blow the place up!
That was my advice.
But after the storm and the earthquake,
after the tactic of the exploding plane
and the strategy of the sinking boat, it looked

like fate and I wanted to say, "Don't you see?
So what if you're a famous biochemist!
Lost with all hands is an old story."
Sure, we're on the edge
of an important breakthrough, everyone
hearing voices, everyone falling

into caves, and you're out
wandering through the jungle
in the middle of the night in your negligée.
Yes, we're way out there
on the edge of science, while the rest
of the island continues to disappear until

nothing's left except this
cliff in the middle of the ocean,
and you, in your bathing suit,
crouched behind the scuba tanks.
I'd like to tell you
not to be afraid, but I've lost

my voice. I'm not used to all these
legs, these claws, these feelers.
It's the old story, predictable
as fallout—the rearrangement of molecules.
And everyone is surprised
and no one understands

why each man tries to kill
the thing he loves, when the change
comes over him. So now you know
what I never found the time to say.
Sweetheart, put down your flamethrower.
You know I always loved you.

Doctor Watson's Final Case

Regarding these most
recent outrages we sincerely hope
there will be no repetition.
Enough damage has been done
although, I must admit, we did not
lack advice, or warning—
twelve, in all, anonymous letters.

Don't you realize there's
a monster at large
in this city
bent on destruction?

But no one knew how long
you'd been nosing around the waterfront
disguised as a gorilla, the same gorilla
found missing from the zoo exactly
one week to the hour before
the night of the crime. "I don't know
where he could have gone," the keeper told
the reporter, his eyes filling up
with tears. "I always thought
he was happy here."

"This man," you said,
catching the orderly by his sleeve,
"died precisely
at the stroke of twelve. Observe
the ash from his cigarette." Naturally
a full confession followed.

"Well, sir, it was all my fault.
I know I should have spoken out
the first night they arrived at the office.
But the sight of blood oozing beneath the door
seemed to awaken murderous instincts.
Then Brezard was gone.
'Are you going to let this happen?'
they said to me.
'Are you going to throw away
the chance of a lifetime?'
What choice did I have
after all?"

"It's reasonable," you concluded,
"because it's true."

Thus we find no necessity
to release at this time
the whole story concerning
the politician, the lighthouse,
and the trained cormorant. I maintain
no one would have understood
in any case.

"On the contrary," you reply.
"There is at least one reader
who would have understood.
There is always one reader
who will understand."

The Blue Histories of the Wind

Yet a little sleep, a little slumber, a little
*   folding of the hands to sleep;*
So shall thy poverty come as one that travelleth,
*   and thy want as an armed man.*
                    —PROVERBS 6:10–11

Our relationship with the world which we entered so unwillingly
seems to be endurable only with intermission. . . . It looks as if we
do not belong wholly to the world, but only by two-thirds; one
third of us has never yet been born at all.
                    —SIGMUND FREUD

1

Again, the ominous sounds of furniture!

Chairs rubbing against the desk.
Books slipping from their places.

By morning
two more pictures have disappeared
into the wall: a landscape
with cows and a mountain;
an old man with a beard.

Out on the lawn I complain to the manager.

"The view is not what I was promised.
The village is impossible to find,
and something is wrong with my room."

"Yes, yes," he replies, "everything
has been taken care of."

2

Often, I unlock
the tiny photograph you gave me.
It grows darker
each time the sun touches it.

My work goes badly here.
Every day things retreat a little further,
and now even the subject escapes me.
Mirrors? Sun spots? Or just ordinary weather?

Ragged ghosts
wander down the paths of misfortune.

Not now, they say. *Later.*

Then everything begins to be the same.

You drift further away
and when you return
you are changed, and then I
too am changed.

3

About the city I can add
little to the other letters.

Today it seems
I have business there.
Addresses and appointments appear
next to my napkin at breakfast,
but if I delay long enough
they are taken away.

Have I told you about the others?

M., who spends all day drawing maps,
and R., who carries a gun and will
never speak to me. Nor can I discover
what they want.

No one goes to the beach any more.
The ocean grows colder and more silent.

Tonight snow is predicted.

What else can I tell you?

4

"No, not *dead*, Doctor. That body
has never been alive!"

Little flames jumped from the electrodes.
He began waving his hands and shrieking:
"This monstrous experiment of yours
challenges the very order of creation!"

Then I remembered
what had to happen next—
villagers advancing into the forest
with their torches and pitchforks, and the monster
stumbling through the mire toward the windmill,
or the quicksand, or back
to the black pits beneath the lab.

"But in whose darkness, Doctor, will we meet?"

Weeping a single tear, he pulled the fatal lever.
"We belong dead."

5

It's like that.
Hard to get in, and hard
to get out again.

Weeks pass, and months,
or so it seems.

From time to time
I hear footsteps on the stairs,
coming up, going down.

Then quite suddenly
after a night of storms
I pick out a description,
two or three possible explanations.

The intricate machinery of the rain!
The erratic, swooping flight of bats!
The sweet, predictable adventure,
plotted out to the end.

And finally a knock on the door.
"I saw the light so I came."

It doesn't matter, I reply.
Nothing matters except
that you've come back.

Tomorrow all these pages will be empty.

6

When the story is repeated
the end is always different.

For an hour everything is green.
Then blue. Then gray.
I walk through it when it's green.
Leaves. Grass. Still water.

Last night I found
I had given up the laboratory,
dismantled the machines,
buried the notebooks.

Though in each was some part
I was sure of.

But what could I ask for?
I never wanted to live here.

If only I could imagine another country!

If only I could think of nothing
but the perfect lives of strangers.

7

Now you lean over your book,
your face falling among the paneled hallways.
Five hundred pages of rooms!
But it's late. It's evening
in all the windows.
As the fire burns,
the pink roses on the wallpaper
shudder and close.
The piano plays an old song
no one remembers. Then
it's too late. The roses
have moved into the windows,
into the tall mirror guarding the desk,
into the white notes of the music,
into the book. Your hand
slips from its place.

8

Snow is predicted.
M. tells me, "After the snow arrives
it will pretend to be everywhere.
No one believes it."

Even my own notes baffle me:
"Three gray geese in a green field grazing.
I always remember that.
I used to love to see it." Or:
"Consider: the blue histories of the wind."

"When the monster saw the first torch,"
M. says, "no part of him
wanted life at that price."

When I took out your picture
you were all but gone,
as if you had not been there,
as if suddenly
I could not be here.

9

On my table: the shape of a window
with a blue jar and a single cloud.
Invisible objects.

Even the weather possesses its spells,
as sleep its divisions and one
constant deception.

I should have known.
I should have expected it.

The tall man who travels,
the armed man who never speaks—
my companions.

Our journeys connect
in this hotel at the edge of water.

Together we walk out
into the winter. Its light
turns on us with a hundred edges.

10

Unfamiliar territory opens around us.
We watch our steps.

We pass the doctor. "What is one life,"
he says, "in the service of those mysteries?
Look at the heart, the heart!"
We pass the old man with the beard.
He says he was your father.
He says, "I am blameless. Let me pass."

The tall companion unfolds his maps
while snow attempts to circle us
with its pale confusions.
And again I hear your voice
returning from some unlikely distance.

Look. When I unfold my hands
they fill with disguises,
all that I have managed to save, all
that I have invented to save us.

This way, the blue wind replies.

The storm divides before us,
closes after us.

This way, this way.

from

Other Children
(1987)

A Night's Museum

FOR JOSEPH CORNELL

William Blake saw an angel
sitting in a tree. Blondin crossed Niagara
on a cable. And Marie Taglioni
for a Russian highwayman
danced on a panther's skin spread over the snow
in 1835. You place one marble
in the glass, one on the shelf beside it.
Five silver thimbles
become a forest, and from the chateau
romantic music exactly
like a dream. You said
you wanted to know somebody who had known Debussy.
"I could have spoken to him
and the chain
would have been established."
Blondin crossed the gorge
a second time, then a third. Many still believed
it had been done with mirrors. "So much,"
you said, "gets by me all the time
in trying to hold onto things." Far above
river, fields, and frozen woods,
against the wind a heavy cable sways.
Behind it, the star charts, the histories
of the sky like
wallpaper. And this cork ball
would be the moon,
and these
are the planets on their strings.

What We Should Have Known

In the movies he looks into her eyes
and knows what they both must feel.
And he's right. She feels it too,
if it's that kind of story. The hotel's
gauzy curtains billow in around them
and perhaps there are fireworks
across the piazza, or the howling
of a wolf far out on the moor.
Sometimes we can tell this scene
is just an excuse for the words
no one could manage to make believable.
I'm sure it will happen again.
Or: *Don't ask me why I mustn't marry you.*
Later, when he stares into the mirror
while shaving, he sees how badly
he's acted, wasting his life
over nothing—flimsy theories
of the perfect murder, or the experiment
that could never be reversed.
Frequently there are flashbacks
to a happier time: picnics on the beach,
boating in the park. At the end
of which he says, "I'd like
to think of you as belonging to me."
She brushes back her hair. The sun
begins to strike the hundred spires of the city.
When she walks across the lawn
we know this is the way
decisions are revealed. The breeze
ruffles her blouse, and her long white skirt
is arranged to catch hold of the light.

For You

FOR JUDY

I don't want to say anything about
how dark it is right now, how quiet.
Those yellow lanterns among the trees,
cars on the road beyond the forest,
I have nothing to say about them.
And there's half a moon as well
that I don't want to talk about,
like those slow clouds edged
with silver, or the few unassembled stars.
There's more to all of that than this,
of course, and you would know it
better than most, better I mean
than any other, which is only
to say I had always intended
finding you here where I could
tell you exactly what I wanted to say
as if I had nothing to say
to anyone but you.

Two Clouds

FOR JENNIFER, MARCH 20, 1977

Smallest breath
on the pillow, we counted
all the months,
first day of spring, first day
of summer, and each night now
as your silence
draws us back to you, here
where these soft leaves are leaning
over a little water
inside this circle
painted on your bed, and that cloud,
that aimless puff, goes on
floating through the same perfect sky.
If there's a secret,
I won't ask.
If there's one good explanation,
I don't want to know.
Your blue eyes
catch hold of everything
that pleases you,
and you know
what I mean when I say, *Look at that!*
That I mean, Look at me.
As if one more reckless smile
would rescue
the morning's gray
indifferent weather, and nothing
would be left to speak of
but this
feathery branch of the willow,

or the shadow of the nest
lodged above it,
or the shadow of the cloud
that sweeps the grass and is gone.

A Familiar Story

When Hansel and Gretel began to eat
the house of bread and candy, an old woman
cried out, "Who is nibbling at my little house?"
And the children answered, "The wind,
the wind, the heavenly wind."

Innocent and clever, they will find the way
back home to their father, and will not blame him,
who twice agreed to send them into the woods.
There was so little to eat, and his wife
reproached him for his weakness:
"Is it better for four to starve when two might live?"

The witch's cottage was a pure temptation,
the children's lie of no importance.
"It is not me," they called.
"It is not me, but only the wind."

That night, they thought they were in heaven.
In such clean white beds
how could they help but believe in kindness?
Or imagine, as they fell asleep,
that they were home, standing together
in the kitchen doorway, the tall pines shimmering
in the sun behind them, and their real mother
kneeling in front of the oven, singing
to herself as she tested
with one finger each new loaf of bread.

On the Island

After a night of wind we are surprised
by the light, how it flutters up from the back of the sea
and leaves us at ease. We can walk along the shore
this way or that, all day. Sit in the spiky grass
among the low whittled bushes, listening
to crickets, to the whisk of the small waves,
the rattling back of stones. "Observation,"
our Golden Nature Guide instructs, "is the key to science.
Look all around you. Some beaches
may be quite barren except for things washed up."
A buoy and a blue bottle, a lightbulb
cloudy but unbroken. For an hour
my daughter gathers trinkets, bits of good luck.
She sings the song she's just invented:
Everybody knows when the old days come.
Although it is October, today falls into the shape
of summer, that sense of languid promise
in which we are offered another
and then another spell of flawless weather.
It is the weather of Sundays,
the weather of memory, and I can see
myself sitting on a porch looking
out at water, the discreet shores
of a lake. Three or four white pines
were enough of a mystery, how they shook
and whispered, how at night I felt them
leaning against my window, like the beginning
of a story in which children must walk
deeper and deeper into a dark forest,
and are afraid, yet calm, unaware
of the arrangements made for them to survive.

My daughter counts her shells and stones,
my wife clips bayberry from the pathway. I raise
an old pair of binoculars, follow the edge of the sky
to the lighthouse, then down into the waves as they
fold around rocks humped up out of the sea.
I can turn the wheel and blur it all
into a dazzle, the pure slips and shards of light.
"A steady push of wind," we read in the book,
"gives water its rolling, rising and falling motion.
As the sea moves up and down, the wave itself
moves forward. As it nears the shore friction
from the bottom causes it to rise higher
until it tips forward in an arc and breaks."
On the table in front of the house
is the day's collection: sea-glass
and starfish, a pink claw, that blue bottle—
some to be taken home, arranged in a box,
laid on a shelf, later rediscovered, later
thrown away, casually, without regret,
and some of it, even now, to be discarded,
like the lesser stones, and the pale
chipped shells which are so alike
we can agree that saving one or two will be enough.

Scene from a Novel

In this scene from the novel
you just started, a father
tiptoes into his daughter's room
to watch her sleeping. All he wants
is to look at her for a moment.
He brushes the damp hair from her eyes,
touches her unfolded hand so that
she murmurs and turns against the pillows.
The room is streaked with yellow
from the night-light. Careful stacks
of books beside the bed, favorite animals
pushed up against the wall,
and the sheets all ruffled and apart.
You know what he's thinking—the apparent
safety of the house, the inevitable damages.
Turning the page, you grow more apprehensive.
Suspecting what will happen
chapters later, you can't help but resent
this cruel preparation. Yet each night
fathers step into such rooms
long after it's time to say goodnight
and feel implicated and afraid.

The Witch's Story

Everything you have heard about me
is true, or true enough.
You shouldn't think
I'd change my story now.
A stubborn, willful little girl
comes sneaking
around my house, peering
in all the windows. She's disobeyed
her parents, who knew
where the witch lived. "If you go,
you're not our daughter any more."
That's what they told her. I have
my ways of knowing. All pale
and trembly then, she knocks at my door.
"Why are you so pale?"
I ask, although of course
I know that too.
She'd seen what she'd seen—
a green man on the stairs, and the other one,
the red one, and then the devil himself
with his head on fire, which was me,
the witch in her true ornament, as I
like to put it. Oh, she'd seen what she needed
to send her running home
but she walked right in, which is the part
I never understand completely. Maybe
she believed, just then,
that she was no one's daughter any more,
and had to take her chances, poor thing,
inside with me. "So you've come
to brighten up my house,"

I said, and changed her into a log.
It was an easy trick, and gave me little pleasure.
But I'd been waiting all day.
I was cold, and even that
small fire was bright, and warm enough.

Night Song

Out in the dark the sound
of water folding and unfolding.

On the kitchen table
plums and an apple.
The chipped white plate.
The studied poverty
of small observations.

Others are now asleep and dreaming
of strangers or the specific
fears of youth that will
by morning have left their
cloudy resemblances.

Night birds and bats.

Then a little music,
far off. Because of it
no one wakes
or changes his mind.

The yellow moon
climbs out of her clutch of branches,
serene and dispassionate,
figure from a story in which
nothing is left to chance.

Touched by that
powdery light, the real
objects of desire
darken and turn away.

The Room

For my mother, Marjorie Young Raab
October 10, 1913–March 20, 1978

Everything has been arranged too carefully.
The way the eyes are closed, that certainty.
I can see it isn't possible to pretend
that the dead are only sleeping.
The way the hands are folded
we don't have to touch them.
When I touched them I knew it wasn't necessary.
I've watched my wife and daughter sleeping.
I've watched you. No matter how still,
there's an imperceptible trembling
accompanies everything that lives.
It's the way a feather sways, that chance.
It's the cloud on the mirror,
that stain. For a while we imagined
our concerns were yours. Is this blue dress
the one you would have wanted to wear?
And these rings, that silver pin?
Is this the music you especially liked to hear?
But the dead among their flowers
have no preferences, and I think
it must be wrong to pretend otherwise,
if only for my sake, and not now for yours.

Cold Spring

The last few gray sheets of snow are gone,
winter's scraps and leavings lowered
to a common level. A sudden jolt
of weather pushed us outside, and now
this larger world once again belongs to us.
I stand at the edge of it, beside the house,
listening to the stream we haven't heard
since fall, and I imagine one day thinking
back to this hour and blaming myself
for my worries, my foolishness, today's choices
having become the accomplished
facts of change, accepted
or forgotten. The woods are a mangle
of lines, yet delicate, yet precise,
when I take the time to look closely.
If I'm not happy it must be my own fault.
At the edge of the lawn my wife
bends down to uncover a flower, then another.
The first splurge of crocuses.
And for a moment the sweep and shudder
of the wind seems indistinguishable
from the steady furl of water
just beyond her.

Listening to a Certain Song

tonight I was reminded of our house in England,
the little record player that always skipped.
Our dozen records seemed such a luxury, although
we had much more back home in Massachusetts.
I don't want to pretend that we were poor.
You read Virginia Woolf and Thomas Hardy.
We argued badly and often about whether
or not to have a child, and when you cried
I talked until you stopped, with nothing settled
and nothing proven except that so many words
might bring us back to the way I thought
our lives should be. Twice it snowed.
Birds nested in the thatched roof. A woman
we never saw again brought us a Christmas tree
with the roots still on it. When we show
the photographs of that house to friends
it's this we talk about—the deer in the woods,
the cow that got loose on the lawn. Remember
waiting once a week for the bus to market day?
Remember when the rented car broke down in Scotland?
How easily that year becomes this landscape
of favorite stories, revised out of habit until
neither of us can tell whose correction
is the truth, or if it really matters.
Friends drove down from London, nervous
and unhappy, their marriage a wreck,
and worse to come. We gathered blackberries
from the hedgerows until the neighbors
must have thought we were starving
and brought us loaves of bread, unable
to make sense of Americans who didn't own a car.

But no one can ever understand why anyone
chooses to live where they're living.
I told the man who sold me rubber boots
that I liked the silence. "Ah yes!" he replied.
"But sometimes the silence can drive you mad."
And we laughed at his dramatic gesture because
the silence was wonderful and no one
either of us had known
had ever gone mad. We bought a chair that broke
and a lot of books we sent home in small, carefully
wrapped packages, and they all arrived.

Other Children

1

When my daughter watched the explosion
of Mount St. Helens on the evening news,
and saw those houses smashed by the mudslides,
she could not have known this wasn't
likely to happen here, and she was worried,
for the first time perhaps, over such concerns—
someone's house crushed and gone completely,
someone's father breaking down and sobbing,
who had just been told for certain what he'd lost.

Nor could she have understood how often
we'd seen that shot, that man
among the wreckage, a broken toy in his hand.
Nor, at three years old, could she
have expected that he was going to cry—
covering his face with both his hands
as if embarrassed by his grief—and then
look up, bewildered, at us.

2

Accustomed to the daily
summaries of loss, it's easy to believe
the news, by definition, happens elsewhere,
and in a world that's always worse
than it is, each day, for us.

But when I watch my wife and daughter
drive off to school, sometimes I can't
help but see myself standing beside
the warped and twisted metals of the car.
Inside, they're looking up
at nobody. And I can't move away
from the edge of this imagining,

where no one calls me,
or comes crawling out of that fire.

3

In Grimm's "The Juniper Tree," the perfect,
beautiful wife wanted a child so badly
she died of happiness when he was born,
and then was buried, as she had asked,
beneath that tree. But the stepmother
envied the boy and one afternoon
when he was looking inside a chest
to find an apple, she slammed the lid
down on his neck, and his head flew off.
Now what will I do? she thought.
She picked him up and set his head back on,
put an apple in his hands, and when
her own daughter, Ann Marie, returned
from school, she said, "Go ask your brother
to share the apple I just gave him,
and if he doesn't answer, box his ears."
The girl went off and did as she was told,
then ran back sobbing. "O Ann Marie,
what have you done? But we will stew him
in the sour broth, and no one will know."
So the woman cut him up and served
that black stew to her husband,
who couldn't help but eat, saying,
"What good food this is! Give me more."
And the more he ate the more he wanted.

4

In the newspapers I read about a father
who put his son in a bathtub filled
with scalding water because
the child needed to be taught a lesson.

So much that seems essential
is simply not included.

And this: in California
a young woman named Betty Lansdown Fouquet
left her five-year-old daughter out to die
on the center divider of the interstate.
Twelve hours later, when the girl
was rescued by the highway patrol,
they had to pry her fingers from the Cyclone fence.
She told them she had run after
the car which was carrying her stepfather,
her brother and sister, and her mother,
"for a long time."

5

But Ann Marie saved her brother's bones,
tied them in her scarf, and laid them
in the grass under the juniper.
All at once that tree began to tremble,
and a bird flew out of the branches, singing
so sweetly no one could resist, even
the stepmother had to go outside
to hear it, and a millstone fell on her head
and she was crushed. From that spot
fire rose. When it was gone the bird was gone,
the brother was restored, and he took his father
and sister by their hands, and they went back
inside the house, sat down and ate their supper.

6

Driving to work one morning a man
sees this little girl running right along
the divider by the chain link fence.
He's half a mile down the road before
he gets angry that her parents would let her
play in a place so dangerous. Some people,
he thinks, shouldn't be allowed to have kids.
Then he can't imagine how she crossed
the lanes to get there, but tells himself
there's got to be an explanation even if
he's now too far away to find out what.
Later, at home, he doesn't tell his wife
the story, worried she might ask him
if he stopped, and he would have to tell her
how he couldn't, not at that hour,
with all that traffic, which she should understand,
but he knows she wouldn't understand.

7

"When I die," my daughter asked me,
"will I still have my fingers?"
I can't remember what I told her.
That day I must have thought
any answer would be sufficient.

Some stories seem impossible
to explain with any other story.
The boy in the bathtub, the girl
running along the divider,
her brother and her sister watching
from the backseat of the car as if,
perhaps, they were the ones who needed
to be taught a lesson. What kind of shape
would hold this, even briefly, all together,
with no magical bird, and without its song?

As my family sleeps I step outside and see
the early morning air glittering
in the arms of the pines, and clouds
lifting from the mountain into a sky
already clear and weightless,
while on the lawn in the frost
each shrub and tree has laid its own
brief white ghost.

8

Let's say the boy survives, is sent away
to live with a family who always wanted
a child to care for. Years later
he receives this letter: *All that I desire*
now in my life is for you to forgive me,
but if you can't I know I will understand.

Or the little girl grows up and marries,
has a daughter of her own and for a time
she's happy, until her husband
leaves her, one morning, for no reason
she can figure out. His note says only,
Got to get away for a while.
Will write soon and try to send some money.
But he doesn't write, and no matter
what she does her child keeps crying
until all she can think about is how
to keep her from crying.

9

It is a long time ago now, as much as two thousand years maybe, that there was a rich man and he had a wife and she was beautiful and good, and they loved each other very much but they had no children even though they wanted some so much, the wife prayed and prayed for one both day and night, and still they did not and they did not get one. In front of their house was a yard and in the yard stood a juniper tree. Once, in wintertime, the woman stood under the tree and peeled herself an apple, and as she was peeling the apple she cut her finger and the blood fell onto the snow. "Ah," said the woman and sighed a deep sigh, and she looked at the blood before her and her heart ached. "If I only had a child as red as blood and as white as snow." And as she said it, it made her feel very happy, as if it was really going to happen.

10

One by one the bones are gathered.
Not even the smallest is left behind.
Such care is taken that when the body returns
it will not lack a finger or a toe.
Mist rises, spreads, and blurs the landscape.
Later it will rain. Later the sun
will rise, the morning's haze burn off, and birds
assemble once again in the juniper. Years
will pass, and the bones will grow still whiter
waiting for the body to come back to them.
Other children will be born, some loved,
some feared. And the parents who loved them
will find their places in the ground beside
the ones who did not, as the wind flutters
the branches of the tree, the birds repeat
their most familiar notes, and some who listen
imagine they can sense a shape beneath
this song, which for a time contains the grief
each believed was his, or hers, alone.

from

What We Don't Know
About Each Other
(1993)

A Crow

Here is the strict, abstract
light of winter. From a bare branch
a crow takes flight, rising
heavily, overcoming
the impossible. Snow
sifts from its branch.
A white shawl.
Thousands of separate flakes.
The bird has moved to another tree,
cawing harshly, though I can
barely hear it, with the windows
locked in place against
the cold. So the mind
remains at a distance
from its concerns,
its uncertain desires—
nothing to think of, or to say,
nothing truly seen until later.

What We Don't Know
About Each Other

In the next room my youngest daughter
is practicing the piano. I don't know why
that halting scale has made me think
of writing to you, after so many years.
Isn't it always the weather one begins with?
Here there is still a little color left,
the bronze of the oaks, pale yellows
of the lesser trees. Three or four
warm days in October are what we believe
we're entitled to, but that turned into a week,
then another, until we felt blessed
and disconcerted. Today the children and I
discovered a small patch of ice
and we were excited to have found it,
bright and brittle, full of shapes.
I walked them out to the bus stop;
they ran on ahead, and back to me.
It was one of those mornings
when you feel the season change, and you think
tomorrow you'll have it again
even more keenly. I remembered others.
I thought of how, looking a long way back,
I expect always to uncover some personal design
in everything. And so it's there,
by chance, by mistake, by necessity.
All the moments that might have gone differently
become the scraps of stories I run through
while falling asleep, so similar
in their melancholy heroism, their few

predictable cruelties. For all I know
you may have given up thinking about me.
For all you know I may have died,
a sudden tragic illness, or perhaps
the time my car spun out of control on the ice.
What they say is true—everything slows down
to a long arc, and though you do the right
or the wrong thing with the wheel, whichever
way you're supposed to turn it, the car
goes on as if you'd been abandoned, or released.
So there was an odd disappointment
plowing into that snowbank, the snap
of the seatbelts telling me I was safe,
then the stupid difficulties of getting out.
Later I could afford to be afraid,
when it didn't matter. Then I just stood there,
looking around me at the fields
and a small grove of pine trees
where snow was sliding off the heavy branches
very quietly and very slowly. That whole scene
was so sharp and certain, so *new,* I thought
I should feel as if I'd been given a second life.
Then would I decide to write to you,
hoping to explain how often I'd wished this
or that day had gone differently, and you or I
had spoken as we never did?
Now she's moved on to a song—"Waltz,"
or "The Three Boatmen." You'd laugh
to think it was a song at all,
but inside those stiff, hesitant repetitions
I can hear the melody she's after. What we know
or don't know about each other—
it doesn't matter, except that I've
moved beyond these careful inventions.

And that young woman you saw this morning
hurrying out of the library, fastening her coat,
looked like me only for a moment. There was
ice on the pathway, the sweet possibility
of snow in the air, all of the necessary
appearances of change—and yet the life
you've taken up to make this letter
could not be my life, just as this voice
was never mine, nor even yours.

Lies

In Sunday School we talked about lies
and if it was ever right to tell them.
What if you could save someone's life?
What would God care about then?
We were in favor of saving someone's life,
though more anxious to defend the lie
and win the argument.
The world outside was quiet.
When the president said we weren't involved
our parents saw no reason for concern.

Later there was the story of the house
and the fire and what you would save
if you could save only one thing—
the cat, the Rembrandt, sometimes
even a grandmother was involved. Then
the lifeboat: how six could live
if one would consent to die.
It was suicide or murder,
all the extremities without detail.

Soon we were told salvation
lay in saying what we really felt.
So men and women explained everything
they'd always disliked about each other,
and some looked farther back
to discover what should be troubling them.
It was necessary to learn how to cry
in front of others who didn't know your name.

Who could excuse anyone else?
We returned to secrets, business trips
to Akron and Detroit when there was no business,
diaries and locked drawers, private correspondence.
And few of us worried about God, having decided
we could forgive ourselves
when the time came for it.

Houses burned in the cities
and nothing was rescued.
Because there was too much to understand
we were told to trust
the experts. We were told
forty percent might survive.
The stories we read had no endings,
just the details of this life
or that one, men and women
who believed that lies sounded like the truth,
or as much like the truth
as anything they could remember.

Learning How to Write

The whole thing looks like things that would show up anywhere around here.

—DEREK, GRADE 5

It's cold outside, or it's dark.
It's raining, or it could be.
Why not begin with that?
In the bright sun the trees
are perfectly still,
which only a moment ago thrashed about
in the storm. Similar things
happen elsewhere. The sky
is a sheet of blue paper, which may lead
to an ocean, or sorrow.
There are streets and pathways,
and people stroll along them.
Or just yourself. Or your father.
It's years ago and he's happy
having learned he's becoming your father.
You see how easy it is. Things
show up, and you gather them together,
things that look like anything
that might be around here.
Now you're walking home from school,
the day the dog chased you
into the street and the car
almost hit you. And it's possible now
to see the funeral, your small coffin
(because, in fact, you were hit)
the way they lower it so carefully,
the way they don't start

shoveling the dirt on top of you
until the family has left.
It's cold outside, and it's dark.
But you can follow them home, you can be
a ghost in the corner of your own room,
and at night you can listen, and find out
how much they really miss you.
And after you've heard enough
you might decide to be back
in your body, waiting on the corner
by the curb, so when the dog comes out
you turn on him with the stick
you've given yourself, except
this time maybe it should be raining,
not hard but steadily, and all the cars
are moving very slowly and very carefully
since at any moment and for no reason
someone might run out there.

The Shakespeare Lesson

FOR JOHN REICHERT

None of the students liked Cleopatra.
    She was selfish, they said, and Antony
was a wimp—because he wouldn't decide
    how he felt, because he ran away,
and couldn't even kill himself.

They were so impatient
    with the languors of Egypt, the perfume
and the barges, those fond little games
    he felt so close to.
Is there anyone you admire? he asked,

himself half in love with Cleopatra.
    Caesar, one student answered,
because Caesar knew what he wanted.
    The sun caught in the smudged-up
panes of glass; he fiddled with the lectern.

Could he tell them Caesar
    was the wrong answer?
Antony, after all, had betrayed the man
    his soldiers needed him to be.
And Cleopatra was foolish, unpredictable . . .

Could he ask them not to feel
    so certain about what they felt?
He said it was complicated.
    Why does it have to be complicated?
someone asked. Is that always good?

And shouldn't they have talked,
    figured out what they meant
to each other? Why does everybody
    always have to die?
Let's look at the last scene, he said,

and saw a stage crowded with bodies,
    saw her body displayed among the others.
How does it make you feel?
    he asked, although he did not know anymore
what he wanted them to say.

The Bad Muse

Calm down. No one's listening. Of course
you have the right to make mistakes.
Say anything you want, any dumb thing
that occurs to you. On the other hand,
it really does look bad, doesn't it?

And if anyone were foolish enough to print it,
scorn and ridicule would be heaped upon you,
upon your family as well.
Think about them, if not yourself.
Someone in New Hampshire or California

is writing the important poem about history
at this very moment. Most of it
is done already. And this person
has had a life of great interest,
full of struggle and incident, whereas yours

is the same old life a thousand people
have had the good sense to keep to themselves.
Who wants to hear about what it was like
to turn forty, or the strange thing
your dog did last week? So relax.

Think of how good it will feel
to climb into bed and turn off the light.
And tomorrow is Sunday. You can read the papers,
go for a walk, cook outside. Friends will drop by.
Why not invite them all to stay for dinner?

And when the conversation gets really lively
and they're nodding in agreement
with everything you say, maybe someone
will ask you to tell that story—you know,
the one about the dog and the squirrel.

The Sudden Appearance of
a Monster at a Window

Yes, his face really is so terrible
you cannot turn away. And only
that thin sheet of glass between you,
clouding with his breath.
Behind him: the dark scribbles of trees
in the orchard, where you walked alone
just an hour ago, after the storm had passed,
watching the water drip from the gnarled branches,
stepping carefully over the sodden fruit.
At any moment he could put his fist
right through that window. And on your side:
you could grab hold of this
letter opener, or even now try
very slowly to slide the revolver
out of the drawer of the desk in front of you.
But none of this will happen. And not because
you feel sorry for him, or detect
in his scarred face some helplessness
that shows in your own as compassion.
You will never know what he wanted,
what he might have done, since
this thing, of its own accord, turns away.
And because yours is a life in which
such a monster cannot figure for long,
you compose yourself, and return
to your letter about the storm, how it bent
the apple trees so low they dragged
on the ground, ruining the harvest.

What He Thought
About the Party

My husband's chief complaint was that we'd included
too many people who believed in outer space.
He made no distinction between those who were intrigued
by the problems of the Hubble Space Telescope
and that much smaller group who personally knew
someone kidnapped by aliens. Outer space
was all the same to him, endlessly uninteresting.
I have to admit I was bored myself
by the Hubble Space Telescope. I kept thinking
of the Artist's Renderings I grew up with, how close
you were to the Martian canals, for example,
with figures in the foreground to add a sense
of perspective and a little drama. But I'm one
of those people who believe any movie
can be improved by including a giant insect.
I like it when the aliens walk among us
and no one's sure they're there, when they take somebody
up in the ship to examine him, but you never really
find out why. They leave so little evidence behind,
and what there is gets covered up so quickly.
Mostly I keep it to myself, these interests.
It's nothing I count on, and you can imagine what he says,
this and that about the world, the one he cares for.
We wash the dishes, make sure there aren't
any more glasses leaving rings on the piano.
If aliens have been around so long
you'd think we'd understand
what they want. Instead we don't even know
if how they're acting is smart or stupid.

When it's time to walk the dog I say I'll take her
because I enjoy going into the yard at night.
The sky's spread out above me, clear and chilly.
Ordinary planes are up there, lights flashing off and on,
and of course the stars, and all the uninhabitable
planets, and then the others, where right now maybe
plans are being made, where everything's almost ready.
No one can say it isn't possible, not for certain.
I like waiting just a moment for something to happen.

The Uses of Nostalgia

1

Twenty years ago there was a life for each of us
to turn away from
or embrace. A song returns to remind me
of what I must have felt,
and when it's over, I play it back again.
Each time it's true.
Don't we look beautiful in the picture
no one ever took,
the clear sky unfurled above us, the wind
ruffling our hair,
everybody's real life just about to begin?

2

I know nostalgia
wants to make the present
feel bereft: a way of pretending,
neither the truth, nor invention.

Homesickness
as a disease; sentimental
yearning for the past.

First love. Second love. All that brilliance
the years have blurred, if not disproved.
Making the big play and winning the game.
Season after season, someone does it.

3

Above us the fan was slowly circling.
It was a room in which others
must have made love often, and sometimes
both of them felt good about it.
As we did just then, our bodies
allowing us the aftermath
that's sweeter than desire—
and a whole day to follow
in which every small gesture
had already been explained.

4

Sometimes I can hear
the teacher in me speaking so passionately
about the world inside a book I'm sure
no one will leave the room
unchanged. Until I notice

who isn't paying attention, disappointed
when it's the prettiest girl
fiddling with her notes, no reader
for the poem so exact
it could make her fall in love.

And I haven't forgotten nights
when desire was an instruction
my body refused to believe.

Then we had nothing that was right
to say to each other.

5

Then it's not the past
I yearn for, but the idea
of a time when everything important

has not yet happened:
love, fame, happiness—
unrealized, yet certain,

like the moment when we take our places
in a theater:
that slow falling of the lights,

that hush
as the unseen curtain rises.

Happiness

I can remember only once feeling perfectly happy.
I was eighteen, a freshman at college.
It was October, and I was sitting on the lawn
behind my dormitory, leaning against a tree,
reading a book. It must have been Sunday.
Leaves covered the grass, though the oaks and maples
were still full of color, and the sky
was that bright and absolute blue
you see in photographs of peaceful country scenes.
The musty broken smell of autumn
floated on the air, that scent like a taste,
like the idea of change. People walked past
on their way to the library, others
slept in the sun, or read their books.
Certainly I had enough to worry about.
I'd made no friends, was not in love, didn't like
my classes. But I felt just then
at ease, and then, lazily, quite
gradually, completely happy—as if that afternoon
might continue indefinitely,
and lead seamlessly into everything
that was going to be possible for me,
which I would one day call my life. No matter
what I thought about it, this would happen,
and I did not have to think about it.
I imagined staying until dark, when someone
might come by to ask what was wrong.
Yet there was nothing I needed to say,
since I had no reason for feeling what I felt,
since the landscape was like a beautiful picture
of where I was, and so, after a few hours,

I got up, without regret, and went back to my room.
This happened, although that doesn't matter
to you, who know about the truth of poems,
how I can't convince you by insisting on the real,
can't persuade you by claiming this I is me, or was.
And yet I am not trying to persuade you of anything.
There is no conclusion, no story to conclude.
And how poor, after all, how familiar
the details seem, without excitement, or surprise.
But I never felt that way again, nor do I expect
to feel that way again, so thoughtless
and solitary, so unaccountably happy.

Magic Problems

The magician saws a woman in half,
pulls a rabbit from his shiny hat.
How did he do it? But we know
our pleasure requires not knowing how.
An amateur in the audience
would be looking for specific moves,
judging the trick on skill alone.
No fun for him, just homework.

When I was young I discovered
a way to prove that God exists.
Just let your mind go back
as far as possible, past the apes
and the volcanoes, past the fish with feet,
back to whatever first made thing
—a big stone, fire, air—you can imagine.
Then you call whoever made that "God."

No one was much impressed by this,
though it was comforting to think of God
inventing the world, not above me
watching what I did.
The magician finds a burning torch
in an empty paper bag—
a good trick, but frightening
if we didn't know about illusions.

Lightning blasts the dead tree—
we're confident it's not a sign.
When the stars assemble into human shapes

we remember their names,
or looking up at them now I know
where I left the book that would remind me.
A stick snaps not far away in the dark,
and because I've seen rabbits

at the edge of this small woods
I call it a rabbit. Then a creaking—
like a screen door being opened
where there is no door—which must be
the weight of a branch
on another branch.
Or a man, trying to stand
very quietly, adjusting his position.

Daily Life

We knew the rat in the crawlspace
was chewing on something essential.
But who'd go down to set the traps?
The house was ours—wasn't it my duty
to protect it? Woodchucks arrived,

nipped the heads off all the better flowers.
Deer browsed their way
through the evergreens. Beside the porch
ants assembled their castles, then moved
into the damp wall of the kitchen.

What fine idea of nature would let me feel
my house might as well be theirs?
By morning, moles had taken over the lawn.
I flattened their little tunnels
and felt satisfied. By afternoon
all of them had been built again.

"When those ants get a taste of this,"
the exterminator told us, "you just watch
what happens." He pumped the wall
full of poison. They wouldn't budge.
"Pinwheels," said the clerk at the hardware store.
"Moles hate those things. Try pinwheels."

The yard was a vast city, the house another.
I considered the advantages of resignation.
I thought of Thoreau in his cabin,

Wordsworth among his daffodils and ruins.
I thought of all the great poems
of sympathetic observation, how my poem
wouldn't be one of them,

though in the end it might still assume
a certain festive air, with many
bright wheels spinning in the breeze
as if some splendid party
had been happily concluded, the children
driven home, only the dutiful father
left out in the evening, smiling at his work.

Stories in Which the Past Is Made

TO MY BROTHER

There would have been a time when I hated you
so completely I'd have thought
nothing could overcome it.
And why was that?—since you shielded me
in the predictable violence of schoolyards,
and told me, once or twice, what I needed to know
before I discovered I'd have to know it.
I wasn't so unwilling
to follow you, whose clothes I grew into,
who had things first and when they were new,
then fought for all the permissions
I'd inherit—the cars and girls, and how late
was too late, or just late enough.
What went wrong between us?
Was there one truly bad occasion?—
or simply the years of ordinary silence,
being apart and coming back
for the celebrations and the deaths.
And then we felt it together:
that need to be friends, although friendship
wasn't what we could have,
only love, the love of restoration,
of repair. So much of the past remained,
and late at night with the house asleep
we found those stories
neither could have remembered alone,
stories in which the past is made,
and corrected, and made again.
And so, my brother—the one they loved
the best, being the first,

the one who died before I was born,
the one nobody knew—
at last we have spoken.

At Evening

FOR MY MOTHER

At first everything reminded us of you.
We couldn't help remembering, wanting
to talk about it together. We understood
this was the way grief works
to return us to ourselves—no discoveries
or revelations, just the old stories
full of incident and detail.

Then your death grew quieter,
a suspicion the world would always seem
vaguely wrong, as when turning a corner
we recognize someone who isn't there.
Or when a storm, pushed up for hours
against the mountains, swerves off
and only the ordinary afternoon remains.

Six years now: marking the time
season by season. So we say without thinking
of the first warm days of spring: "Like last year."
And when we decorate the tree: "Last Christmas . . ."
Left out, you move farther away,
no longer even the image of yourself
but an idea of absence, sad and abstract.

Around the house you never saw us living in,
the ragged music of the crows does not
remind us of what you might have said.
It's summer, the heavy peonies shredding
out onto the grass. And at evening
the light is dense and delicate,

the mountains arranged in a purity of blue
tier after tier. So that a sense

of comfort begins to include me,
without acknowledgment. A last crow
clatters back into the pines.
One by one: fireflies, stars.
So many flickering emblems—and this stillness
in which remembering might not be an obligation.
You would know what I mean,
you would have known what I mean.

Marriage

Years later they find themselves talking
about chances, moments when their lives
might have swerved off
for the smallest reason.
                              What if
I hadn't phoned, he says, that morning?
What if you'd been out,
as you were when I tried three times
the night before?
                              Then she tells him a secret.
She'd been there all evening, and she knew
he was the one calling, which was why
she hadn't answered.
                              Because she felt—
because she was certain—her life would change
if she picked up the phone, said hello,
said, I was just thinking
of you.
              I was afraid,
she tells him. And in the morning
I also knew it was you, but I just
answered the phone
                              the way anyone
answers a phone when it starts to ring,
not thinking you have a choice.

What I Forgot to Mention

Things fall apart.
First a chair, then a table. We can see
the roof needs replacing,
the garden's overgrown. How easy
to think only of obligation,
to talk for hours and say
nothing surprising. One afternoon
a neighbor's tree is struck by lightning.
It falls. And the maples shelter tiny insects
chewing on their tender, folded buds.
Then it's summer. All the convenient emblems
—flowers, seasons, rivers—
shrink a little in the heat, that cruel
weather I wasn't going to speak of.
But you, dear, what did you remember today?
Oh, the mind leaps backwards
and we shrug it off: just one flower,
nameless, bent toward water.
We were walking by and you picked it
out of sympathy. Or you let it stay.
Long ago the petals fell off.
Why think of it? That stain of purple,
so small it could mean anything.

The Secret Life

1

In a garden at evening a man
walks slowly among the shadowy flowers,
feeling that familiar melancholy
as it surrounds him—still, full of promise.
Far off a woman might be singing.
Where had he heard that song before?
Someone in a story, following the pathways
of such a garden, might also
stop to listen, and perhaps
instead of sorrow he could feel
a sudden, incomprehensible happiness—
as though the whole world
were watching him, keeping quiet, and waiting
for him to understand it . . .
The sky is clear, lit up with stars,
and now the air seems cold enough
to imagine frost by morning, to imagine
how the flowers might be damaged.

2

When he knew the cancer had returned
he wanted things to be quiet.
He sat on his porch, looked out at his garden,
and finished his work. This is what
the newspaper tells us: Raymond Carver,
Writer and Poet of the Working Poor, Dies at 50.
At dinner before a reading six or seven years ago,
I remember how he turned the wine glass over,
turned it over before the waitress
could ask if he wanted anything to drink.
It was such a definite gesture.
It said: That's not in my life anymore.
Then he ordered a large Coke, lit another cigarette,
and we went on talking. Hours before
he died, the obituary reports, he spoke to his wife
about how much he admired the stories of Chekhov,
whose death he had described with such care
in the last story in his last book of stories.
Olga went back to Chekhov's bedside.
She sat on a footstool, holding his hand,
from time to time stroking his face.
"There were no human voices, no everyday sounds,"
she wrote. "There was only beauty, peace,
and the grandeur of death."

3

"What do you want for your birthday?"
I asked my father, making our drinks before dinner.
It was a question he always answered
with a shrug—another shirt would be fine,
another pair of socks.
"What I want you can't give me,"
he replied, and paused—
"To be ten years younger."
In a few weeks he'd be seventy-four.
Why ten? I wondered. Why not fifteen,
or forty? Was he looking
back to some moment in his life
I knew nothing about? He'd never tell me,
even if I asked. I gave him the drink.
"But nobody can do anything about that," he said,
as if, already, he'd said too much.

4

In Chekhov's "The Black Monk," the young student,
Kovrin, knows what he sees is an illusion—
that legendary monk who sweeps across the world
every thousand years, who chooses him
to counsel and support. Yet what a pleasure
to talk all night of beauty, and the idea
of genius, and the object of eternal life!
Then one morning his wife awakens, terrified
to find her husband laughing
and gesturing passionately into the air.
Yes, he admits. It appears I must be mad.
Don't be afraid, she cries. All this will pass . . .
But Kovrin turns against her
after he is cured. He becomes reasonable,
sad, and mediocre. Years later,
in a small hotel by the sea,
where the air is warm and tranquil,
Kovrin steps out onto the balcony
and hears a woman singing
something familiar—a melancholy ballad
about a young girl listening in a garden at night
to sounds so beautiful and strange
she knows they must form
a sacred harmony, not to be understood by others.
Suddenly Kovrin feels that joy he thought
he'd lost forever, and at this moment
the monk returns. There was no reason,
he says, for you to stop believing in me.
But Kovrin cannot answer, his mouth
has filled with blood, and his hands flutter
helplessly before him, as the black monk whispers

that he has always been a genius,
and that he is dying only because his body
can no longer contain that genius.

5

"I think," Chekhov wrote to his friend
Suvorin, "that it is not for writers
to solve such questions
as the existence of God, pessimism, etc.
The writer's function is only to describe
by whom, how, and under what circumstances
the questions of God and pessimism were discussed."
I don't think my father was remembering
a secret life. I think ten years ago
must have looked like a time
when he wasn't afraid of dying,
when he hadn't started to worry,
each day, about how painful it might be.
Although I'm sure of this,
I don't want to believe it.
But could I ask him to imagine anything less real
than pain? And what would that be?
Beauty? Peace? Any kind of grandeur?
When all he wanted
was not to feel what he was feeling.

6

At times I imagine a voice,
not yet any person's voice.
What can it describe? A clear sky
full of stars. Or sunlight
on the frost in a garden. And the sound
of water or of trees in the wind which make
a sound like water. Then the light
finds a room where two people
are talking. It enters as if it were
another person who had arrived
unexpectedly. What were they saying?—
these two who are quiet now, watching
the light, which has made their silence
singular, like nostalgia
or regret. One I recognize
as myself, while the other,
who is not yet my father,
leans forward, trying hard
to listen, or about to speak.

7

In the woods darkness arranges itself
into shapes. I walk outside, and the cut grass
makes a wide avenue among the pines,
which, in a dream, or a story,
might lead somewhere.
Someone could stand here for a long time,
letting the stillness of the evening
include him, feeling that affection
we feel for the world
when it lies at peace around us.
And when he understands he must be waiting
for something to happen
that cannot happen, he turns
and sees the lights of his own house
not far away, the familiar pattern
of the windows, which he will look up into
as he walks back, thinking
he could still be anyone
out there with the darkness around him,
until he reaches the door, until he walks inside.

from

The Probable World
(2000)

Why the Truth Is Hidden

First, I'd like to thank God,
said the pilot,
shot down and rescued. Later

after the big game the best player
says it again, and the announcer
nods. It's right

for the winners to be grateful,
and useful for their thanks
to sound like modesty, since America

doesn't like a man who's good
at what he does and wants
to talk about it.

And the losers? They know
His ways are dark, His path
difficult. They understand justice

isn't always what it seems,
or else they couldn't, who've lost
the most, bear it. Surely

God was wise not to speak
to us anymore. After all,
what did that accomplish?

Endless arguments
about who knows who's right.
Centuries of murder.

Every religion, Pascal said,
that does not affirm that God
is hidden is not true.

That's what, in His disappointment,
He must have decided. Stay back,
keep quiet, let them come to you.

Love

In a sudden rage a man kills his wife.
Then he drives back to his house.
There's no getting away from this, he thinks.
He hadn't tried to hide anything.
The police will show up soon.
He has a gun, so he tells himself
he should do it now, outside on the lawn.
Or he could get back in the car,
drive around for a while. It's hard to decide.
His dog is out there, certain
something is wrong. No,
he's not going to shoot the dog.
His heart's already broken,
knowing he's killed his wife
whom he still believes he loved, knowing now
he's a man who could do that kind of thing.
The dog comes over to him.
He thinks the dog wants to help
and it breaks his heart again
to feel he'd been kinder
to his dog than his wife, or at least
kind enough to deserve this trust,
this affection. Love? he thinks.
Would that be going too far?
He walks inside, sits down,
puts the gun in his mouth.
But the dog scratches at the door,
keeps on scratching until
he gets up, lets her in, half-aware
he's made a choice.
How can he kill himself in front of his dog?

He strokes her head.
Good girl, he says, and then
other things no one says to a dog.
If only she would go to another room.
But she won't leave, and no matter what
he tells her, she refuses to be comforted.

Respect

A latticework of trees at dusk, silhouettes
of sky shading upwards into the darkest blue.
I'm thinking of Frost stepping out of his cabin
to watch the snow falling, evening coming down.
I've seen the place, walked around the chair
he wrote in, felt a suitable respect.
I've seen the film his publishers made
where he wanders off to chop some wood
as if that was what he always did
before beginning a poem. When in fact . . .
But why should we care about that?
So what if he was a terrible man. So what
if Philip Larkin hated everybody, and wrote
his friends to say how much
he hated his other friends, and finally
all the world except, perhaps, the Queen.
He knew how to keep it from his work.
I'd like to believe he found a place that mattered
among those words, but what do I know?
For him it may have mattered less and less.
What's to be done with all the rubbish
of a life when you know so little
can be made memorable? They got famous
and mean. They were rude at parties
and lost their friends, or couldn't be sure
if they had or not. They got old
and were afraid. Now I'm imagining
Frost opening the door to see
snow coming down fast into that field,
and thinking of nothing new to say.
But by then the world should look

the way you've written it.
So what if the world changes. So what
if you suspect, late at night when you can't
drink yourself any closer to sleep,
that all your bitterness adds up to nothing
but more bitterness, and those few books
are what you used to be.
So what if that's sad, and it is. So what
if there's no other way to end.

American Light

In those days a traveler prepared himself
to be astonished. There were wonders
in every direction—the mountains *stupendous,*
the precipices *lofty,* the waters
profoundly deep. No one settled for anything
less than the sublime. Don't fool yourself.
You also would have cherished the Idea
of Nature, how inside it a better self
lives to repair whatever might befall you—
any calamity, any disgrace.
This is the world without encumbrance,
that famous light trembling across it.
Consider the hush of the storm on the far horizon,
that abandoned boat by the shore. And further west—
woods *of the dimmest shade,* the solitude
utter and unbroken. Now you've climbed
some great cliff. You're feeling
like a new man, overwhelmed
by everything you can see, certain
this world will never fail you.

A Small Lie

1

The reporter expected the place would be
"sinister beyond words," and it wasn't.
It seemed "harmless." The barracks
were painted "a pleasant soft green."

So many rooms, emptied of their cries,
turn into dingy schools,
the bunkhouses of a summer camp . . .

Decades later, the guard they captured
was a frail old man, who claimed
he'd been somewhere else, working at a desk.
When the survivors recognized him,
he said they'd made a terrible mistake.

"Do you know what this is?"
the mugger asked my friend, showing him a gun,
and after he'd taken his money
he said, "You know, I wasn't going to hurt you."

Many had been told
they were just going off to work.
How could they have believed it?

2

But now we think we've learned
something about evil—how it likes to appear
ordinary, like anybody's grandfather.

Sometimes the kid next door
buys a rifle and kills his family.
The neighbors are shocked,
then admit he'd always been quiet
and a little strange. Now they can see it,
how he wasn't like the others,
their own sons and daughters.

"I saw him coming," my friend was saying,
"and I should have turned away.
But I kept walking."

And as he walked he told himself a small lie—
Of course this isn't going to happen
—which was what he'd told himself
many times before, when it had been the truth.

All Day

Others cannot escape their subjects.
History, injustice, whole countries
gone begging for a song. For them: the silence
of high places, the risks of an open field,
and that shattering light in which
a man might find a way
beyond himself, each new burden becoming
another piece of luck.
                    Who can be content
with the sadness of the past? Here:
the bright swerve and rise
of a small fire, the smell
of woodsmoke—I knew what I'd be reminded of,
how many rooms and nights would appear,
how the word *sadness* would have to be
resisted.
          Just beyond
this house with its curling tendril of smoke
there's a meadow in which deer gather,
eating their way through the afternoon.
When a dog barks they look up,
wait, and return. Birds
continue to sing.
              Somewhere
heroic deeds have already been performed,
significant acts of betrayal.
In the squares of besieged cities
the wounded are still crying out.
Some ask for help, but others
beg their friends to stay away, the shells
keep falling, and truly

nothing can be done.
　　　　　　　　　So all day
passes, until at evening
the field seems empty, the dog
is asleep, the fire is ash,
soft and delicate. You might
even kneel down and touch it.

The Lost Things

In the attic or cellar, back in some drawer, way back
on the top shelf of somebody's closet
were the stamp albums and the baseball cards,
both cap pistols in their leather holsters.
In our house nothing was actually lost,
even if we didn't know where to look.

So those guns rusted, and the pages of books
turned brown. No one had taken proper care,
but that wasn't the point. Permanence
was never the point. Instead:
the desire not to feel regret.
When the time came,

the house up for sale, every closet
open to inspection, I took what I thought
I wanted, even if not to decide
was what I wanted, to leave things
in their places, let the pictures crack and the mice
chew at the spines of the Hardy Boys and

Tom Swift and His Submarine,
Tom Swift and His Rocket Ship,
Tom Swift in the Caves of Nuclear Fire.
Not selling them or throwing them away,
not saving them either. The way we think
anything can be remembered, if memory
is like opening the right drawer
or taking a box down from a high shelf
for no particular reason.

Why Tragedy Is the Wrong Word

It's too grand for the worst
that happens to most of us.
We suffer heartaches, die in disasters.
Think of the truck out of control
on the thruway, or the bridge
about to collapse. Think of the terrorist
planting his bomb.

Not one of us
is spared such imaginings.
Touching down, the plane explodes.
A few survive; hundreds
are scattered across a cornfield.
Then *disaster* sounds insufficient, even cruel.

Then it seems right to forget
the old definitions: how tragedy required
stature and knowledge,
how it depended on a hidden weakness,
an inevitable fall, how it made
death look noble and necessary.

Years Later

Sometimes my father returns
in a dream, backlit
in a room that belongs
to none of our houses. Although
we do not speak, I know
he hasn't died. That was
a mistake, my error. And always
I'm grateful to understand this.

*

Now I can start over.
Now I can begin imagining you.
In those beautiful black-and-white photographs
you're young and handsome, posing
beside some monument, or proudly
holding up a string of fish.
Here is the lake in New Hampshire,
early morning with the mist in place.
Here's your rusty green tackle box
and that old wooden rowboat.
You slide it into the water, adjust the oars.
When you reach the place
in the cove among the waterlilies,
you cast into the fog, watch it rising
around you until all the cottages
emerge in bright duplicates,
still guarding their sleepers.
Then the first breeze begins
rearranging those reflections, and your boat,
unanchored, drifts through them.

You open the thermos of coffee.
It's Saturday. This is happiness, you think.

*

If we could never speak to each other
whose fault was that? In every family
someone is more silent, and the conversation
circles around him, the jokes
turn against him, which he permits.
I always thought you knew
what you wanted your life to be.
And when you got it, you couldn't
imagine anything else you might need,
anything you should have needed.
Or you kept it to yourself.

*

It's Saturday, and you
haven't caught a single fish,
but that doesn't matter.
You give yourself another hour.
Even then it won't really matter.
Your wife is still asleep. Perhaps
I'm back there also, still asleep.
But no—this should be earlier.
Now you can see the cornfields
behind the cottage. You can hear the crows.
A screen door opens, and she steps out
onto the porch in her bathrobe.
She waves, but not to call you in.
Everything looks so clear.
I should let you go.

*

In another dream
soon after my father's death,
I found myself walking through a town
I'd never known, down a worn cobbled street,
and I saw him in the back of a wooden cart.
We noticed each other without astonishment.
How are you? I asked. Meaning:
How does it feel to be dead?
I'm fine, he answered quietly.
But I could see this was awkward for him,
and I thought perhaps he wasn't
permitted to speak of his new life.
He was almost gone when I asked,
And is she there with you?
How is she? Fine, he replied.
She's fine too. How strange, I thought
as I began to wake—
that he would say so little, that I
could give him so little to say.

In the Garden

Before the Fall
Adam and Eve tended the garden,
pruning and ordering,
and when they slept
the lavish trees and shrubs grew
just enough to require attention.

They didn't call it work.
It was what they did,
being part of a plan
they couldn't see the shape of.
But they must have felt
how pleased God was to observe them.
One day was what they had, the same day,

in which they worked separately.
At night did they dream? I think
they could not have dreamt,
since the past was the same
as the future—neither hope
nor despair, only tendrils

and branches, the heaviness
of flowers leaning over the path
that led from the man to the woman
and which, each day, needed to be cleared.

"My Soul Is a Light Housekeeper"

Error in the printing of the line
"My soul is a lighthouse keeper,"
by an unknown female poet

Bored with the high drama of watching,
I see myself bound always to your absence,
sending out my pure circle of light so you
will know where I am, and how close
you might come to disaster. Imagine, love,
the tedium of this watch. On almost every day
nothing happens. And isn't it wrong to yearn
for a great storm just to feel important?
I'll let you go, then. Why shouldn't my house
be my own, and my soul its keeper?
This work I needn't take so seriously
since I've learned what pleases me, the light
of late afternoon through that window,
the intricate cobwebs I won't disturb.
I know you don't want to think of me
not always thinking of you, brave and imperiled.
I'm sure you'll write to say: *How can you change*
so completely? You're not the woman
I thought I knew. And I'm not,
but understand, dear, it wasn't such a great change.
Imagine you could have seen that side of me
at the beginning, when we walked
for hours along the shore, and you were so certain
I was yours just because you loved me.

Great Art

There's so much I don't want to look at,
big religious scenes especially,
big historical battles,
almost anything, in fact, containing
large numbers of people.

Three or four people—that's the right number
for a painting. Then you can think
about what they might mean to each other,
why they're standing around that beach
at sunset, walking toward that mountain.

Or they're at home: a woman sewing, a child
playing, a dog, a man at the door,
much more ominous, I'm sure, than the artist
intended. And I like that, imagining
this isn't what I was supposed to feel,

the way I'm pleased with small imperfections,
stains and wrinkles, erasures particularly,
where you sense the artist changing his mind.
And sometimes a shape's been painted over,
although the ghost of it remains.

In Vermeer's *Girl Asleep at a Table*
she leans on one hand, dreaming
perhaps of love. Behind her there's a mirror
in which nothing is reflected. Once,
X-rays have shown, this was a portrait of a man.

And we would have understood, given
the conventions of the time, he was the subject
of her thoughts. Why take him away?
It's better, I want Vermeer
to have decided, not to show that much.

Let her keep her dream to herself.
Let the light be our secret.

Another Argument About
the Impossible

Even if we agree in principle that a poem can be
about anything, you still want to claim
it cannot include space aliens,
since by their very nature (you insist)
they are silly. And even if belief
is a subject that's stood the test of time,
a poem about a man who believes in space aliens
will be a poem about a man who is either
silly or demented. Belief requires
a world of consequence all around it:
men, women, nature, history, and so on.
Reality, of course, is another matter, but see
what happens (you continue) when these
are put together, as in: "My work
concerns the nature of reality, belief,
and space aliens." It would be different
if we knew they were there, but we don't,
and a poem cannot afford to adopt
such a wait-and-see attitude toward the world
which, after all, has provided so many
more compelling subjects. No (you conclude),
not even a poem that argues against them
can survive their presence,
not even if the aliens never appear,
never do or say anything, never threaten us
with their neutron blasters, never steal our women
to populate their planet, not even if their ships
remain hidden, and we are never taken up in them
to be probed and instructed, dazzled and released.

Hunters

This last cold winter killed the flame bush
at the edge of our meadow, although I'm sure
those hungry deer helped it along.
They should have eaten less.
Next year if the snow's as deep
they'll have nothing. But they're all
so tame and stupid they stand around that field
in the middle of hunting season, as if they trusted
the signs that say Keep Out. A farmer
in Vermont used to paint COW on the sides
of his cows and they still got shot.
And I've heard that serious hunters
dress in camouflage, figuring that even a red vest
could be some drunkard's idea of a deer.
Somebody's out there in the cold with a gun
thinking, Man and Nature, Mortal Combat,
and then a flick of white—
how could he tell it was laundry?
Or his friend unwrapping a sandwich?
It's the price we pay for woods nearby.
I'm not complaining. So many others
have it much worse all the time. Step out
on the street at the wrong moment
and it's over. You were in their line of fire,
or you looked like somebody who'd just
burned them on a drug deal.
Or maybe they were driving by and since
you were nobody one of them said,
"Let's blow that guy away." It was bad luck,
though if they'd known you, and if
they'd needed one, they would have found a reason.

Permanence

I can't remember how old I was,
but I used to stand in front
of the bathroom mirror, trying to imagine
what it would be like to be dead.
I thought I'd have some sense of it
if I looked far enough into my own eyes,
as if my gaze, meeting itself, would make
an absence, and exclude me.

It was an experiment, like the time
Michael Smith and I set a fire in his basement
to prove something about chemistry.
It was an idea: who I would
or wouldn't be at the end of everything,
what kind of permanence I could imagine.

In seventh grade, Michael and I
were just horsing around
when I pushed him up against that window
and we both fell through—
astonished, then afraid. Years later

his father's heart attack
could have hit at any time,
but the day it did they'd quarreled,
and before Michael walked out
to keep his fury alive, or feel sorry for himself,
he turned and yelled, I wish you were dead!

We weren't in touch. They'd moved away.
And I've forgotten who told me

the story, how ironic it was meant
to sound, or how terrible.

We could have burned down the house.
We could have been killed going through
that window. But each of us
deserves, in a reasonable life,
at least a dozen times when death
doesn't take us. At the last minute

the driver of the car coming toward us
fights off sleep and stays in his lane.
He makes it home, we make it home.
Most days are like this. You yell
at your father and later you say
you didn't mean it. And he says, I know.

You look into your own eyes in a mirror
and that's all you can see.
Until you notice the window
behind you, sunlight on the leaves
of the oak, and then the sky,
and then the clouds passing through it.

My Life Before I Knew It

I liked rainy days
when you didn't have to go outside and play.
At night I'd tell my sister
there were snakes under her bed.
When I mowed the lawn I imagined being famous.
Cautious and stubborn, unwilling to fail,
I knew for certain what I didn't want to know.

I hated to dance. I hated baseball,
and collected airplane cards instead.
I learned to laugh at jokes I didn't get.
The death of Christ moved me,
but only at the end of *Ben-Hur.*
I thought Henry Mancini was a great composer.

My secret desire was to own a collie
who would walk with me in the woods
when the leaves were falling
and I was thinking about writing the stories
that would make me famous.

Sullen, overweight, melancholy,
writers didn't have to be good at sports.
They stayed inside for long periods of time.
They often wore glasses. But strangers
were moved by what they accomplished
and wrote them letters. One day

one of those strangers would introduce
herself to me, and then
the life I'd never been able to foresee
would begin, and everything
before I became myself would appear
necessary to the rest of the story.

The Invisible

At every point
the great dazzle of the world
shines through it,

distracting you, as you should
be distracted, since all this
is life, whereas the invisible

is one of the shapes
life never chose.
Or could not hold for long.
And so, at moments,

it trembles into sight—
as the tip of a swaying branch,
or a road unwinding into the distance,

leading, perhaps, to a mountain
where you never lived
alone in a cabin, happy
to keep the fire going
on a chilly day.

And what you might have dreamt there—
has it entirely slipped away?

Moonlight makes a bed.
Arranges its thin sheets.
Now a woman is taking off her clothes.
A man is opening a door.

How pale they look—
almost transparent.

Outside, the wind stirs and rises.
A branch scrapes against the roof.
Another road unfolds into another night.

The Pole

We were back at college, young again.
She was someone I yearned for
throughout the spring
of my senior year. In the dream
it was evening and she was having dinner
with her friends when I appeared
at the door and waved to her
until she came out onto the porch where I
was standing with a long wooden pole,
maybe five or six feet high. I said
I had brought it to her because
I'd heard she was going rock climbing.
Yes, she said, but you don't need
poles to go rock climbing. Which I knew.
From the beginning of the dream I'd been aware
that was the case. Which meant
nothing would happen between us,
although the strangeness of my gesture
didn't seem to trouble her. She smiled at me.
And in the dream I remembered where
the pole had come from. I could see it
leaning against the wall beside the blackboard
of my third or fourth grade classroom,
a long pole with a metal hook on top
used to lower the shades that covered
that room's many tall and empty windows.

Fragile

Sometimes the world insists
that we think about our places in it—
how fragile they feel, each one
nudging the next. So many inscriptions
already written. Here lies.
Beloved of. Remembered forever.

Fragile: shattery, shivery, gone.

When you're old enough to have felt
(alone, at night)
the kind of pain a few pills
won't take care of,
then maybe you've wondered—

If I died now, what would I leave behind
that would hurt me, what secrets
that would change the minds
of those who loved me?

Think of the man with his hidden shelves
of pornography. He knew he was dying.
He left it that way. He didn't ask:
When shall I destroy all of this?
Who shall I turn myself into?

Brittle, delicate, severable.

Like a leg, or an arm, any part
we can lose without losing ourselves.
Like an exquisite object whose beauty
is blended with the fact
that it isn't meant to last.

All afternoon the sky is full
of enormous clouds, ominous,
mutable. Yet the rain holds off.
We go out to play tennis,
return to eat dinner.

Whatever allows us to be here
thinking as well as we can
we're ready to praise.

Emily Dickinson's House

"It is true," Emily Dickinson wrote
one day, looking out
of her window, "that the unknown
is the largest need of intellect,
although for this no one thinks
to thank God." Almost all my life
I've lived not far away,
but I've never been to her house.
I don't know if her desk
is near a window,
or what she might have seen
through the wavy glass: trees, sky,
another house, the familiar
facts of the world
which she knew must be resisted.
Or learned so well
their strangeness is restored
each time we look: maple and elm,
clouds or sun, then rain,
the neighbor's house (a man inside
reading a book), and then
the unseen moor, and the narrow wind
that sweeps across it.

False Nocturne

Learning how to play the piano, I favored
the most melancholy pieces
because they were slow,
and my hesitations blurred
into the semblance of feeling.

In the music we listened to at school
we heard donkeys descending
into the canyon, followed by a storm.
As if the point of art
was to make us think of something else.

Anxious to step outside
my parents' lives, I was unwilling
to give up anything I actually owned.
Tacked to my desk:
a picture of a monk

ringing a bell in his garden
on a cloudy autumn morning.
At twenty I was determined
to be unhappy, or to sound that way.
But what do I know now

about that moody young man?
How easy to make him look foolish,
who taught me, even then,
how I'd learn to change my mind.
Who kept in his notebook

the story of the piano student
who asked her teacher,
Should I play in time, or in accordance
with my feelings? And he replied,
Why not try to feel in time?

The Questions Poems Ask

Watching a couple of crows
playing around in the woods, swooping
in low after each other, I wonder
if they ever slam into the trees.

There's an answer here, unlike
most questions in poems,
which are left up in the air.
Was it a vision or a waking dream?

You decide, says the poet.
You do some of this work,
but think carefully.
Some people want to believe

poetry is anything
they happen to feel. That way
they're never wrong. Others yearn
for the difficult:

insoluble problems, secret codes
not meant to be broken.
Nobody, they've discovered,
ever means what he says.

But rarely does a crow
hit a tree, though other, clumsier birds
bang into them all the time, and we say
these birds have not adapted well

to the forest environment.
Frequently stunned, they become
easy prey for the wily fox,
who's learned how to listen

for that snapping of branches
and collapsing of wings,
who knows where to go
and what to do when he gets there.

My Spiritual Life

Nothing mysterious ever happened
in our church. Those suspicious transformations,
wine into blood, spirit into flesh,
were comfortably symbolic. Scrubbed clean,
our windows let in the cold New England light.
White clapboards, white walls, a cross
without Jesus, an altar like a lectern.
The year my father was deacon, my mother
sliced the squares of bread for communion.
She said it did nothing for her.
She disliked being told she was a sinner,
resented the assumption that she needed
to be forgiven. Sin was for the Catholics,
she said, and the Episcopalians, who might as well
be Catholics, except they were richer
and had to have a more impressive church.
I never took Sunday School seriously
after I learned we wouldn't be graded.
Something like that would happen eventually,
but then, being dead, we'd understand
what now we couldn't possibly understand.
So it was foolish, my mother thought,
to worry too much about heaven,
especially if so many were going to be excluded,
having chosen one of the wrong religions.
Faith looked a lot like believing
you were right, or your parents had been.
The sun slammed in through those tall, clear windows.
Our minister explained that we were good,
but could be better. Think about it,
turn it over in our hearts. Finally God would decide.
Week by week we were on our own.

The Best Days

FOR JUDY AND JENNY

It's hard to be happy, harder still
to talk about it. Walking together
through these intimate woods, the coins
of light scattered all around us,
it's enough to praise the weather. No need
to disentangle what we feel
from what we think. Or even
to acknowledge the world, not far away,
assembling its important troubles.
The best days, like this one, float
at the borders of our lives, as unremarkable
as light, or the fluttering of leaves.
We know we can't live here.
Perhaps the hermit, having turned his back
on us all, thinks he lives here.
Or the saint, forever trusting
in another life. But we don't envy them.
At evening they must sit down alone
to bless their hunger,
which, perhaps, also makes them happy,
then uneasy, as if they had betrayed
some hard allegiance
to feel this way, the way we feel.

My Life at the Movies

Village of the Damned was the movie I'd chosen
for my first date with Emily, my first
date ever, as well as my last with Emily.
It was a good movie—children with supernatural powers
turn against their parents and take over the village.
But I kept remembering how embarrassed I'd felt
telling Emily on the phone that we'd be going
to a horror movie. Science fiction, I thought
immediately. God, that sounds so much better.

Then there was *The Wreck of the Mary Deare*
with Barbara, who showed up late, so we missed
the credits and the opening scene, and never
went out again. Later *Hour of the Wolf* with Wendy
and Max von Sydow as a demented artist
who must stay awake all night to fend off his demons.

These were not, I can see now, the very best choices.
Certainly they failed to create a comfortable
romantic mood. At least with *Blow-Up*, Nancy and I
had the mystery of the end to talk about.
What does it mean when the photographer
walks away and vanishes, like the body
he'd discovered in the park? That was the Sixties,
a good time to discuss illusion and reality,
an easy time to favor illusion. When we got stoned

and watched *A Night at the Opera* it was amazing
to see how much was going on. Groucho,
we agreed, was a genius, like James Joyce,
in fact very much like James Joyce.
Our teachers were resistant, failing to grasp
the necessary connections. Was Stephen Dedalus
like all four Marx Brothers, or only Groucho?
It was so difficult to explain. We cited
Baudelaire, mentioned the limitations
of rational thought, and were given extensions.

Movies, of course, were much better
than rational thought. Plus they had music.
How could I drive off down the highway without
the right song in my mind? How could I
break up with Nancy without seeing it played out
on the screen: a crane shot, lifting me up
and back and away in one long sweet and floating glide.
Then a slow dissolve. Or the final frame
frozen into significance. Of course

it didn't happen that way, and now
I don't remember the truth. Instead
I think of the last scene of *La Dolce Vita*—
Mastroianni on the beach, so handsome
and anguished. A young girl at the water's edge
calls to him, but he can't hear what she's saying.
Then he smiles and shrugs
as only he could shrug, as if to say he knew

that whatever lost part of his life
she represented, it was too far away from him now.
Knowing that, he could only smile
and shrug, which meant: What can I do?
We can't take the world
too seriously, no matter how lovely
you are in your white dress this morning.

Vanishing

First you worry that you'll never get
what you want, later that you'll lose
what you have. In between
for a time you just trusted
the course of your life, assumed
things would fall into place.
Most of them did. But now,
not quite all of a sudden, every new pain
is a sign, then a promise.
Even if you didn't take death seriously
when you were young, you understood
that was the story. Your kids
leave home, your dog sleeps most of the day.
Letters arrive wanting to know
if you've planned for the future.
You walk out on the porch:
there's a field, then a mountain,
so familiar you have to look hard.
The letters say, It's never too late.
All things vanish. You know that.
All the things you love
vanish. Can you love this idea?
Is that the task? you think. To try?